Judith Wermuth-At

When Someday Is Today

This remarkable and rich memoir, for all its specificity and descriptions of land-/cityscapes in far-flung locations, tells a modern version of the age-old tale of migration across political and cultural boundaries and realms of faith. As someone who has moved in many of the same circles as the author in Sofia, Munich and New York though neither journeyed as widely, nor ever lacked a valid passport, I am deeply impressed by the vast gap in experience of travel and the naked vulnerability of refugee existence. Striking is also the sense of purpose of a young mother who sets out to escape an oppressive, homogenizing political system in the mid-1980s, as well as her own perseverance and that of her two sons in pursuing their dream of freedom, tolerance and a better future. Akin to how the author meticulously prepared a musical performance as a violin prodigy in Bulgaria five decades ago, she seemingly cannot stop seekingùwhether on route in Central Europe, Israel, Minnesota or West Bengalùthat precious moment when the world she inhabits (or instrument she plays) produces, as she succinctly puts it: "the response I wanted". Indeed, the one unsurprising thing about this autobiographical account is the destination, in that she eventually finds herself settled in an exceptionally cosmopolitan portion of Manhattan, a few blocks from the UN headquarters.

Kjell Engelbrekt (Professor at the Swedish Defense University and at Stockholm University; Lifetime Member of the Swedish Royal Society of War Sciences and the Swedish Foreign Policy Society)

Judith Wermuth-Atkinson

When Someday Is Today

Hologram Of An Immigrant's Journey

LIT

Cover: Drawings by Calin Trenkov-Wermuth

This book is printed on acid-free paper.

Bibliographic information published by the Deutsche Nationalbibliothek
The Deutsche Nationalbibliothek lists this publication in the Deutsche Nationalbibliografie; detailed bibliographic data are available in the Internet at http://dnb.dnb.de.

ISBN 978-3-643-91372-2 (pb)
ISBN 978-3-643-96372-7 (PDF)

A catalogue record for this book is available from the British Library.

Flössergasse 10
CH-8001 Zürich
Tel. +41 (0) 76-632 84 35
E-Mail: zuerich@lit-verlag.ch https://www.lit-verlag.ch

Distribution:

In the UK: Global Book Marketing, e-mail: mo@centralbooks.com
In North America: Independent Publishers Group, e-mail: orders@ipgbook.com
In Germany: LIT Verlag Fresnostr. 2, D-48159 Münster
Tel. +49 (0) 2 51-620 32 22, Fax +49 (0) 2 51-922 60 99, e-mail: vertrieb@lit-verlag.de

Contents

Letter to the Reader

Dear Reader,

Long ago, in the 1990s, I wrote a memoir about growing up under an authoritarian regime, about having been a silenced writer, a dissident thinker, a member of a persecuted spiritual movement, and about escaping through the Iron Curtain, together with my eight-year-old child, while being forced to leave behind my older son. My book, entitled *Näher an die Ferne* (Closer to the Distance), was published in Munich in 1999, for the tenth anniversary of the fall of the Berlin Wall and of communism. At that point, I was living in the United States. I had married (again), I was teaching literature, both my sons were well and managing to make the best out of any opportunity they were given. I worried about my students, about my husband's health, and, like some other immigrants, I had almost forgotten that I had ever had another life. Or perhaps, I wanted to forget. Until one day an e-mail popped up in my inbox – an invitation to participate in an international symposium at the University of Nottingham; the theme was "Writing under Socialism." Images, memories, thoughts – all started surfacing in my mind, like ghosts from a very distant past. I was not really a writer "under socialism:" the communist regime, under which I had lived, never published anything I wrote, except my translations. But I had indeed written a book about life under communism and about escaping from Bulgaria – later, when I was living in Munich and I was free.

I accepted the invitation, and I was moved that there were still people – academics, publishers, authors – who cared about researching and analyzing the history of this dark period in the 20th century – a period the millennial generation knew little about. But was all that in the past? The symposium was eye-opening. I realized that I could not leave my past behind because authoritarianism was the present of many, and because freedom of speech and democracy itself were so fragile that different societies had still to fight very hard to protect them.

The collection of essays and research papers, entitled *Writing Under Socialism* was published in 2011. It included my essay "Meeting Myself at

Nottingham". My journey back into the past began. And so did my thought-journey into the present.

Refugees and migrants have been vilified both in Europe and in the United States for many years. The refugee crises beginning in the 2010s have become great challenges for democratic leaders. Citizens living in free societies often have only abstract notions about what forces refugees or migrants to leave behind their homes, families, and livelihoods, what motivates them to escape their countries, to emigrate, to risk their lives and the lives of their children and to accept an uncertain future. What are the hopes and dreams of migrants? Where do they feel at home? What do refugees think about the places they escaped? What lessons does the past hold for the future?

Today, we need to remind ourselves of what a society under authoritarian leadership looks like – the suppression of dissent, the lack of freedom of expression, the ideological manipulations of people's intellectual, artistic, spiritual and religious life, the internment camps, the forced party membership, the fear of persecution – the list is long. In Eastern Europe, a whole generation has grown up without the Iron Curtain. But what does the world look like at the end of 2020? We see a current trend for Russia and China to push for their models of authoritarian governments. We see that Russia has directly threatened democracy and tried at every turn to undermine faith in the institutions that underpin it. We cannot but ask the questions: What would the world look like if Putin manages to keep restoring old or creating new authoritarian regimes? What will happen if he continues to invade territories with "little green men" in Europe, or if he continues to back authoritarian and corrupt regimes in the Middle East? What would Europe look like if Victor Orbán of Hungary continues on his path toward an "illiberal democracy", if the AfD wins in more regional or national elections in Germany, or if Poland's conservative right-wing party PiS continues to undermine the rule of law? What would the life of Belarusians be if Lukashenko remains in power? What will the future of Hong Kong be, considering China's successful efforts to eliminate the one country-two systems model? How eroded would Bulgarian society become if there is no end to the pervasive graft observed in the country? What will life be like wherever democracy fails, and authoritarians and extremists prevail?

Contemplating the political events we witnessed over the last decade, and in particular the politicization of the refugee and migrant crises both in the U.S. and in Europe, as well as extremism, dictatorships' brutalization of their populations, and the threat to democracy itself, made me go back to the memoir I published in the late 1990s. I translated my book from German into English, and I also wrote a second part for the revised English language version – from the perspective of the past quarter of a century. I felt compelled to leave an authentic personal testimony that could help many in engaging with the political and social challenges related to forced migration in their effort to understand better the experience of a refugee, of a migrant.

I sit at home in isolation now, because of a terrible pandemic that has plagued the whole of humanity. I observe the political events around the world and the developments related to the recent U.S. elections and I think how fragile democracy is, how quickly civil liberties can be undermined. For they are not just to be achieved. Rather, they are like beings, whose existence is entirely dependent on our vigilance, on our awareness, on our constant effort to protect and to defend them. So, I write this letter, addressed to you, my reader – in hope that the memory that is written down survives, and that understanding the experiences of the past could help coming generations mold a better future, by considering the devastating consequences for humanity of any potential possibility of a turn towards authoritarianism, wherever that may be.

Judith Wermuth-Atkinson

New York, November 2020

Part I

PROFUGA[1]

To my Father

CW '97

The Scent of the West

The Little One was exhausted. He only wanted to sleep, and he curled up on the seat. It was just the two of us in the compartment. He fell asleep. Quiet as usual. Without asking. Without knowing. He simply trusted me. Outside the window there was nothing to see. Only dark uncertainty. The windowpane did not matter. Nothing was transparent. Outside, there was nothing. Everything was in me. The thick darkness.

The Little One on the seat. A tiny, fragile body. Thin and helpless. My son. My baby. I had him with me. His little hands. His pale face. I was able to touch him, to caress him, to kiss him.

I had only him.

I sat in the nothingness of that night, my nose pressed to the cold pane of glass, paralyzed with fear. I had just severed myself from my previous life. I had rejected and renounced it. My previous life. With the speed of an express-train I was heading away from the thirty-four years I had lived, and my inside tore apart and bled. In my possession I had a backpack, three wild chestnuts, and my child.

Only the one.

The other one was staring at me through the kitchen window of our apartment when I turned around to look one last time. He did not wave, he did not cry. He just stood there, his nose pressed to the cold pane of glass, paralyzed with fear.

I shouldn't have abandoned him. It still isn't too late. There is still time. I could still get off the train before the border. I could be with him for ever. Especially now, when he is still so young. To hell with all plans. I just want to hug you, my darling. My boy!

He knew everything. That I would try to escape. That probably I would never come home again. And he said "go!" He was only ten.

A month ago, unexpectedly, I got my chance.

In our family, there were always troubles with a travel permit. My father was German. A German Jew. After the war two of his brothers emigrated to Israel, a niece lived in the U.S., a cousin in Australia, and another one

---

1 *f.* of profugus: Latin for refugee, fugitive, or one who escapes, who wanders, who is unsettled, exiled or banished.

in Germany. We were receiving letters and gift packages from all around the world. If one of us wanted to fill out the application form for a travel permit, it would have been enough to enter the U.S. and Israel in the column *Relatives and Acquaintances Abroad*, in order for the State Security to pass the verdict – "suspicious." My mother, though, did manage to get a travel permit for a business trip to Western Europe in the '60s.

When my mother was young, there were five men, medical students, among her friends. One of them later became brother-in-law to the notorious Todor Zhivkov.[2] This man tended to avoid contact with old friends, especially with those from an "unsavory" milieu. Despite that, he turned out to be my mother's "connection."

The *Connection* was a widespread phenomenon in those days. A life's ambition. The art of mastering all problems. Through a *Connection* it was possible to secure a place in a kindergarten for one's child; to be accepted in the "*special school for gifted children*;" to be admitted to the university, or to receive special privileges during the mandatory military service. Instead of getting up at half past four and marching on command or being perpetually tormented by some sort of survival training like all mortals, one could be appointed librarian, musician, dancer or singer in the so-called *Construction Troops*[3]. Strangely, this general category included numerous folklore ensembles and other cultural organizations of the army. Through a *Connection* one could later also get a good job with as little to do, and as much vacation, as possible. For good behavior, one could possibly also be sent on a business trip to the West. Those who were really ambitious were even able to make a career with the help of a *Connection*. For that to happen, however, many other criteria had to be fulfilled. In any event, the existential question in those days was not *to be or not to be*, but "what connections do I have," or "whose guy am I?"

---

2 Todor Zhivkov (1911-1998). General secretary of the Bulgarian communist party and head of the People's Republic of Bulgaria from 1956 until the fall of the Berlin Wall and of communism in 1989.

3 The Bulgarian *Construction Troops* originated in the compulsory labor service established by the government in the 1920s for the purpose of building roads, railroads, and industrial enterprises. Although these troops were organized in military units, they were controlled by the Ministry of Construction, Architecture, and Public Services and received almost no military training.

For its part, the *Connection* was very clever – always able to calculate precisely whom, in what way, and to what degree, to help, and always knowing how to take advantage of the situation. When the time came, it demanded repayment. *Eye for an eye* turned into "favor for a favor," you scratch my back, I scratch yours. Usually, the *Connection* was fat and powerful, liked wine and good food, and was called "our guy." And "our guy" would eventually say: "let's see."

The first time my mother was denied a travel permit, she went to her *Connection* and complained. After she was told "let's see," she was asked what "guarantors" she had.

Three party members had to vouch for everyone who wanted to travel to the West, no matter whether the applicant was a party member or not. One of the guarantors had to be a neighbor, another one a co-worker, and the third a friend or acquaintance. At least one of the three was supposed to have known the person in question since their youth. It was difficult. My mother was not very popular in the neighborhood. She was an artist, came from a once-bourgeois family, had divorced her first husband, eventually married a Jew, was beautiful and never able to shut her mouth. At work, her colleagues envied her, because of her talent. So, her hope was in the friends from the time of her youth. They had always been there for her. She must have been charming and lovable as a young girl. The old friends then thought of the past and that she was not really "dangerous," and decided to help her. So it was that in June 1964, a member of our family was allowed to travel abroad for the first time. One month later the scent of the West reached us.

When I was little, the West smelled to me like oranges.

Every year, in December, my uncle would send us oranges from Israel. My very first idea of freedom was having an orange plantation. A bit later, my image of the West changed its contours. I was receiving hand-me-down clothes from my cousin in America on a regular basis. That was another world. It was the colors that impressed me the most. Until then, I knew only bleak, fading colors. When I received the first package with clothes from my cousin I was so fascinated by the fresh, strong colors that I said I wanted to be green, like my new dress.

…

I was about six when I discovered my father's photographs. Papa on a horse, Papa in front of amazing Gothic buildings of a kind which I had never seen, Papa with a top-hat and a cane, in a very elegant car. So I asked him to tell me about his life. My favorite bedtime stories were the stories about my father's life. With time, my imagination created pictures of Berlin, Paris and London, of the life in his home country – Germany, of the organ-grinder on the street, of the streetlights in the night, of the Alps, of the Rhine. And also, of the war.

Then one day I found his library. Bookshelves concealing some secret that I badly wanted to discover. The Cyrillic and the Gothic scripts. These were two different worlds.

When my mother returned from her first European trip, she brought home the world. First, she opened her suitcase, and we were intoxicated by the scents of coffee, chocolate, and perfume. She also brought me a doll. A Sicilian girl, in folk costume. The doll could open and close her eyes and say "Mama." The only thing I had played with until then was an old, tattered rag doll, which I always wanted to dress because I couldn't stand her naked. I gave my new doll the name *Gina*, put her on the shelf over my bed, and never played with her in my life. She was only supposed to tell of that unknown magical world. Then Mother started telling us about it. She had brought back dozens of brochures, catalogues, photographs, and postcards, and she was so knowledgeable in the areas of art and history that she could talk captivatingly for hours about each single street, museum or castle. She told of her trip again and again. All her life.

...

Things were different with me.

After I graduated from high school, I wanted to try to go to study at a university in the former GDR.[4] Western Germany was out of the question. In those days there were no international exchange programs with Western countries open to students. Only some carefully chosen graduates were able to go abroad on a specialization in particular fields. To be approved for such specialization one had to be either already a party member or at least an outstanding Komsomol functionary during the time of her/his graduate

4 Former East Germany, officially German Democratic Republic.

study. Failing to meet those criteria, as an alternative one still had the option to offer her/his services to the State Security, if one was willing to do it. Thus, I could consider only the GDR.

It was my father who took the first step in that direction. He went straight to the embassy of the GDR, met with the Ambassador and told him that he was of German origin and wanted his daughter to study German literature in Germany. The Ambassador expressed his astonishment about my father's initiative very politely and sent him away in an even more polite way, explaining that "such things are not to be arranged so easily." According to him, I was supposed to begin my study at a Bulgarian university and then, maybe later, I could apply through that university to be accepted in a program in Germany.

However, I was not accepted at the university immediately. My parents suggested that they could send me to the GDR with the idea that once I was already there, I could try to register as a student. No one among our friends and acquaintances understood what kind of utopia this was, and we set off to organize another trip – this time mine. This time we had to find a bilateral connection, one that could be useful in East Germany too. A friend of my mother's, who was a historian and had professional contacts in the GDR, expressed her willingness to travel with me. She knew the president of Humboldt University and thought that through him she might be able to "arrange" a study place for me at that particular university. The situation was tricky though. In order to travel with her to Germany, on my way to Berlin I was supposed to pick her up from Belgrade, where she was at an academic symposium.

This was in 1974. To obtain a travel permit to the former Yugoslavia was as difficult as to obtain a travel permit to the West. Usually, people from Bulgaria had to travel to the GDR through Romania. My mother tried to solve this problem too but, this time, no one wanted to help. I was too young – which to the authorities meant that I was potentially adventurous, full of energy, or in other words dangerous. I realized I had no right to make choices or decisions about myself. I might have had wishes or dreams, but I was not allowed even to try to fulfill them. Nevertheless, once again things worked out. Eventually, as usual, my mother found someone, who was willing to put in a good word for me, even though he hesitated for a long time. Our neighbors in the village where we had our summerhouse were very good friends of my parents. They were extremely nice and intelligent people who had found their way to prosperity in communist Bulgaria. The husband was a well-known doctor and the wife worked as a high-level specialist at the Institute for Literature at the Bulgarian Academy of Sciences. During the times of communist upheaval someone from the family of the husband must have given a partisan a piece of bread. Because of that person, our friends could enjoy the so-called *privileges of Partisan-helpers* – a formal definition of a privileged status that was to be found pretty high up on the list of privileges. The two very talented and very charming sons of my parents' friends had graduated from the elite English Language High School, where students were accepted exclusively on the basis of having a recognized *status of privilege.* At the time we became friends with this family, both their sons were studying at the famous Diplomatic School in Moscow. Luckily, these friends of ours knew somebody who was a big fish in the passport department of the Ministry of the Interior. Our friends introduced my mother to this person. Then she invited him a number of times to dinner and eventually I received a permission to travel through the dangerous city of Belgrade. I was also told explicitly that once I was already in Germany, I would have to find a very nice present for Uncle Tosho – the person who helped. For a very long time we knew the guy from the Passport Department only as Uncle Tosho, for he was not supposed to give away any more information about himself. I did not manage to arrange to study in the GDR. Nevertheless, I learned a lot during this first trip of mine.

In Belgrade my mother's friend, the historian, introduced me to a colleague of hers who was from Germany. From West Germany. He was a professor of the kind I had imagined German professors of the Enlightenment.

When I was little, a number of Germans, for whom my father was interpreting, visited our home. I was always most impressed by the fact that they were completely relaxed when they had a conversation. But this was long before. Later, my father was forbidden to invite businesspeople to his home privately. The German professor I met in Belgrade was interested to hear about my country, about me, and about my family, and he seemed to be quite well informed about political and social issues in Bulgaria. I talked to him about things I had never before spelled out. To me, our conversation was like some sort of a confession, in which, for the first time in my life, I put into words my socially determined inferiority complexes. The professor said he wanted to help me. And he kept trying – for seventeen years. At the time, this wonderful man, who had the humane attitude of a free Westerner, represented my only hope in the world out there, the world behind the Iron Curtain.

During an interrogation in the State Security which took place about a year after this ill-fated trip I was asked what the professor really wanted from me.

"You don't want to make us believe that he was talking to you just for fun, do you. What methods did he actually use to win you over to the side of the enemies? Or, perhaps, he liked young girls? And do you really believe that he would invite you to Germany if he didn't have his own hidden agenda? Oh, come on! Are you honestly that naïve or do you think that we are that stupid?"

Everything that one believed in had to be destroyed, no matter if it was God, or a person, or anything else. The world had to appear unsafe and dangerous, so that one would crave peace – the peace of mind that one could have when one felt safe. Only then could the regime offer us the *system* as a desirable alternative. That alternative consisted of less than ten commandments: If you belonged to the *system* you would know how everything else works – according to order, with no surprises.

My transit visa (or rather the stamp on the sheet of paper attached to my ID) allowed me to remain in Yugoslavia for forty-eight hours. On my way back to Bulgaria I decided to visit a friend of my parents in Novi Sad. The finality of my returning was depressing. I had no idea if I would ever again be able to get out of Bulgaria. Was I supposed to give up my dreams forever? It was as if I was claustrophobic. My thoughts became dramatically distorted. I needed to think about all this carefully again. Did I really want to go back at all? This was how I was confronted with the idea of escaping. At that moment I knew only that I needed more time in Yugoslavia to think. In my feverish excitement about finding a way to extend the permit for my stay in Yugoslavia I came up with quite a childish plan. I had ulcers at the time. I pretended that I had terrible stomachache. My host called a doctor who said that I should stay in bed and prescribed a very strict diet. He also wrote a note for the border authorities that I could not leave the country on the predetermined date because of health reasons. The complete nonsense of this plan became clear to me only when I found myself one day sitting in the bathroom of our friend's apartment and chewing on the few macaroons I had bought in Berlin and I was still keeping in my suitcase, because I couldn't stand the oatmeal prescribed by the doctor any longer. The macaroons, however, were soaked in pine shampoo that had run out of a broken plastic bottle and spilled in my suitcase. I sat there at the edge of the bathtub and stared off into nothing. My mouth was full of pine shampoo foam and I couldn't ask anybody for advice, nor could I take any action. It was hopeless. I wanted to have normal food again and I gave up. I was nineteen.

...

Soon after I returned to Bulgaria, I was invited to the German embassy – the West German. The professor had kept his word. Upon his recommendation, the cultural attaché wanted to discuss the options for me to receive a scholarship to study in West Germany.

The embassy was located far from the center of the city, in a very pretty neighborhood, on a small street named after Henri Barbusse. It took me a while to figure out where this street was for. When I was young, there were no city maps in Bulgaria – maybe so that the enemy could not figure out the location of something or other.

I went three times to the place where the embassy was and pretended that I was taking a walk. A militia man was always standing in front of the embassy and I was afraid to even walk on that side of the street. I was just observing him, and I realized that he was always there and took no breaks. My heart was beating like mad and, already by the second time I went there, I was terribly afraid that he might have noticed me. Imagine… Visiting a Western embassy… At the gate stands *Our Guy* who watches that an innocent young girl does not fall into the claws of the danger of becoming a spy, the danger that was waiting in ambush inside the embassy. We all grew up with such exciting stories.

Private individuals were not allowed into Western embassies. Thus, I had to come up with some idea. One morning I went to the embassy again and this time I went straight to the militia man. The militia man was the first authority in any official building. He represented power and felt accordingly all powerful. He was not only supposed to take care of law and order, but he also had to scrutinize the people who were going there. In order to get the appropriate permission to enter some office, people had to explain to the militia man their respective affairs in detail. Luckily, the militia man did not even think that I would dare to come to the embassy on private business. He never asked about my name, which alone already sounded suspiciously foreign. He asked only who had sent me there. "The Academy of Sciences," I said. It was not even completely untrue, for I was working there at that time. The militia man rang the bell, the gate opened, and I was just about to commit my first crime, as the authorities described this visit later. Inside the embassy, however, no one attempted to recruit me as a spy. We discussed the different possibilities to study in Germany and I left with a number of Reclam editions of German literary works which I received as a gift. Later, when I was called for an interrogation in the State Security the agents were appalled that I had not realized how, with these books, the Germans had tried to make propaganda and to influence me. Through Goethe, Heinrich Böll, and Thomas Mann!

The German authorities were fully aware though of how things worked in Bulgaria. I was told very plainly that initially I should apply only for a short-term language school grant, so that "both sides could see how exactly I was going to get a travel permit." Whichever legal way for travelling to the West I might have chosen I might have become suspicious not only for the Bulgarian communist regime but also for the West German authorities, even though I clearly wanted a one-way ticket. The German embassy started inviting me to different cultural events to which I went several times, together with my father. We were both surprised to see many prominent figures from the artistic circles at those events – artists, composers, and musicians. Apparently, the authorities had given famous cultural figures the special privilege of having some access to Western foreign offices in the country.

Michelangelo

In the ’70s, Bulgaria embarked upon a new political course on the domestic front. It was decided to win the intelligentsia over to the side of the government, instead of denying and condemning their existence.

Until the late ’60s, the intelligentsia had been considered the most dangerous social stratum in Bulgaria. People were denied the right to information through the media. The Bulgarian broadcasts of the BBC, Deutsche Welle, Radio Free Europe, and The Voice of America were jammed through special radar systems. The international news in the Bulgarian press was reduced to a minimum and the information it contained was heavily censored. Works of “decadent” philosophers such as Nietzsche or Freud, or albums with reproductions of Munch, Chagall and Salvador Dali, could not be bought anywhere. It was hard to get access to them even in the big university libraries or in the National Library. To get hold of such books in a library, specialists needed a letter from their employers confirming that they had to work on a related topic. This, however, certainly did not extend to students. Young people were not supposed to be even exposed to “decadent” culture, and, of course, most of human civilization apart from Marx and Engels was considered “decadent.” Under the slogan of “avoiding the corrupting Western influence,” the regime was doing its utmost to hinder people in their thinking process. Nevertheless, the cultural situation changed with time. In the ’60s, a cartoonist known under the pseudonym Karandash (which means *pencil* in Russian) printed cartoons in the pages of the weekly comic Stârshel (Bumblebee), portraying American soldiers in Vietnam drunk on Coca-Cola. In the ’70s, there was already enough Coca-Cola in Bulgaria and people knew exactly how drunk one could get on Coke. There were also enough people who knew what was being published in the rest of the world. Even though the information about world politics and events was still scarce, Western culture gradually began to make its way through the Iron Curtain and was comfortably settling among both educated and more ordinary people in Bulgaria. These were the times of the Beatles, of jeans and Coca-Cola, of Russian dissident literature, and of translating contemporary American and Western European writers. The wind blowing from the West could no longer be stopped. In the beginning of the ’70s, even the government realized that people could not be prohibited from thinking. Especially not the thinkers. Thinking, however, could be dangerous, if it were out of control. And so, the regime needed to come up with something.

If you quit forbidding a child to do something, it will quit doing what’s forbidden of its own accord. This was one of the greatest political discoveries in communist Bulgaria. Intellectuals were to be given a chance. The ’70s turned into a period of chances. Some of the poets, writers, and artists who, like “other-thinkers” (if not dissidents), had been sentenced to internal exile and sent to small provincial towns, came back to the capital. They were “rehabilitated” and they were offered relatively good jobs, social housing, trips abroad, and even prizes. Some of these people persisted in the way they were thinking. Others became obsessed with the idea of seizing the chance of their lifetime, not realizing that they would have to make compromises in exchange for this opportunity. What mattered to most of those people was their natural human desire to develop and to express themselves as artists. People say that Michelangelo would have been a great master even if he had no hands. But not every man is Michelangelo. At that time, artists in Bulgaria were given their hands back. This was probably the only way to prevent the birth of an undesirable phenomenon, namely “closet art.”

. . .

I have often asked myself why there was never “drawer-literature” in Bulgaria. At least not in the form we knew it from the Soviet Union. We had no dissident or immigrant literature, and no underground universities as in Poland. Once in a while, good journalists appeared in the Bulgarian broadcasts of the BBC, The Voice of America, or Radio Free Europe. The only major writer, who had settled in London after he escaped from Bulgaria, and who was working on a book about his country, was jabbed with a poisoned umbrella, probably on behalf of the Bulgarian government. A few days later he died in the hospital from an unidentifiable poison. *Reports on Bulgaria in Absentia* was the title of the book by Georgi Markov. And in absentia, he was sentenced to death.

Ambition was the most powerful weapon in the hands of the communist ideologists. Particular emphasis was put on controlled development of the new generation. As under any dictatorship, the Bulgarian regime established a whole system of different mechanisms for manipulating the intellectual development of young people, in this case, in the spirit of the communist ideology.

Children were obliged to join different organizations very early on, so that their upbringing was entirely in the care of the Party. However, the real bargaining with moral values began with the entry exams for the elite "special schools for gifted children," the foreign language high schools, and later also the universities and other institutions of higher education. Universities drew up long lists with privileges that guaranteed acceptance. On the top were the children of the "active fighters against fascism." This was a title which decorated only the very big communists – the partisans and their accomplices, who had been involved in the socialist coup of 1944. The remaining student places were divided among the other privileged categories according to strict quotas. Nevertheless, every year a few normal kids were also able to compete in each discipline. They could make it only if they had the best possible results on the entry exams and the highest grades in their high school diplomas. There were many gifted young people who had successfully taken the entry exams several times and were still not accepted as students. To be able to study at all, many had to choose a major in which they were not at all interested, simply because fewer of the "chosen" ones had applied for it. Later, at university, the struggles were for stipends, exchange programs abroad, and, after graduation, for the best jobs. The system simply had a monopoly over the better chances for the future.

...

I was lucky. Because of my personal circumstances, I almost completely escaped being thrown into the mill of the system. When I was little, my mother, my grandmother, and my older sister were, in turn, taking care of me, so that I never had to go to a public kindergarten. I was going only a few times a week to a private German kindergarten organized secretly, despite all existing laws prohibiting any private businesses, by a nice sweet German lady in her small one-bedroom apartment. Later, I was constantly absent from school, because I was a sickly child and was frequently ill. Eventually,

I graduated as a private student from the Music High School, where I spent the last five years of my school education, in order to have more time for practicing. I played the violin and I spent most of my time alone with myself and my music. Gradually, I developed as an outsider, which turned out to be a great advantage in the society I am trying to describe, for I was almost out of reach for the ideological machinery.

Pater Noster[5]

I cannot remember exactly when I became aware of my relationship to God. There was no particular emphasis on religion in my upbringing, since my father was Jewish and my mother Christian. Even my sister and I were different in that respect. She was the child of my mother's first marriage and was baptized when she was a baby. I, on the other hand, was the Jewish kid. What our parents did teach us was enormous tolerance. All religious holidays, which under communism were not supposed to be celebrated, were simply days we looked forward to in our family, when Mama and Papa did everything possible to create a really festive atmosphere. However, somewhere in the back of my mind, there was Grandmother's Christ icon, which she kept in a small dark niche built for that purpose into the wall of her bedroom, with the vigil oil lamp underneath. There were also the sound of the Orthodox church-bells, and the Sunday service, to which Grandfather used to take me from time to time, in absolute secrecy. People who tried to give their children any religious education were persecuted. Therefore, every time when my grandfather took me to church, he would tell me that we were going to the post office. One day, though, a neighbor was talking to my father on the street and mentioned the post office. "The old grandmas in the post office cross and *god* themselves," I remarked innocently. Back then, I did not even know the concept of *praying* and thus had to come up with a word for it myself. "The post office is where you go to send letters and packages," Papa corrected me; "what you mean is a church." The woman looked at him with astonishment and asked: "How would she come to think of a church?" I insisted that I was right though, and I described precisely where the post office was. I was thinking of an old church nearby, which was in the middle of a pretty little circular park. So, my father was exposed in front of the neighbors, and my grandfather in front of my father.

...

In those days, it was difficult and dangerous to practice any religion in Bulgaria. All believers were aware of that. At the same time, this

[5] Latin for Our Father, The Lord's prayer.

awareness helped people of different religions to understand each other better. Generally, Jews, Christians and Muslims respected one another. That is, until the regime came up with the idea that, according to Marxism-Leninism, at the stage of a "developed socialist society" the people had to represent a "homogeneous atheistic nation." In the spirit of this rushed homogenizing of the nation, the government started a malicious campaign against all ethnic and religious minorities in the '70s that ended with the forced assimilation of the Turks in the mid '80s. Splendid mosques, which were among some of the most precious architectural monuments in Bulgaria, were closed and partly destroyed or burned down. The Bulgarian Muslims, who were partly ethnic Turks, were no longer allowed to practice their religion, to speak their language, to keep their Turkish names or to wear their *shalvars* in public. Those who did not want to change their names knew that they would be fired from their jobs. People were harassed, threatened and forced to live under enormous pressure. Some were even shot at. The regime stirred up hatred and fanaticism, nationalistic passions, and conflicts through which they could manipulate the whole population of the country. The radio broadcasts in Turkish were discontinued. Previously, schools in regions where the Turkish minority was predominant taught Turkish also. Now this was forbidden. Bulgarian Turks and Bulgarian Christians were setting each other's houses on fire, and children and old people on both sides were murdered. Turks could no longer marry Christians and pregnancies resulting from mixed relationships were doomed to be terminated.

My boys' pediatrician was a nice young woman whom I had befriended. When she was still a student, she had fallen in love with one of her classmates who was Turkish. After they had been together for about three years, she became pregnant. The young man's father threatened to disinherit him and to banish him from the family. The old man suffered a lot because of his son. The young doctor had refused to change his beautiful Turkish name. He was working in a big hospital in the capital, Sofia, and they could not simply fire him as they were doing with people in smaller towns in the country. Instead, they stopped the pension of the father, who lived in a provincial town. Without any income, the parents were left to starve for a few months. In the end, the son "re-named" himself from Erol to

Emil, but he continued feeling guilty for the suffering of his parents. At the same time, the father of my friend, the pediatrician, warned her that her application to become a Party member, which she had just submitted, would never be accepted if she were to give birth to the child of a Turk. The two young people loved each other and did not want to sacrifice the baby. However, they were living in communist Bulgaria. Perhaps not even Romeo and Juliet would have dared to marry under these circumstances. My friend brought the baby into the world as a single mother, and her boyfriend married a Turkish girl, to please his father. Eventually though, the couple restored their relationship, but this too caused great disappointment and sorrow. All involved had to lie, including the one illegitimate and the two legitimate children who had now been born.

Through systematic propaganda most Bulgarians were finally convinced that the Turks had forcefully converted Bulgarians by gruesome means six centuries earlier. Thus, it was now the Turks' turn to be converted. About six centuries later! Archives of schools, hospitals and other public institutions were systematically destroyed, so that no Turkish names could be found any more and the nation could attain its artificial homogeneity.

...

When I was thirteen, I fell and had a concussion. I was supposed to stay in bed in an almost completely dark room and was allowed neither to read nor to listen to music. However, a woman who was my mother's acquaintance and lived nearby visited me quite often. Every time she came, she wrote down one particular thought in my notebook. I did not have to read it but I could deliberate on it until this woman visited me the next time. This is how I learned about a philosophical and ethical movement founded in Bulgaria by Petâr Dânov around 1910 and known as the Brotherhood of Light. As soon as I was back on my feet, I wanted to learn more about this school of thought, and I started reading books about it. The lady who came to visit when I was ill would tell me about the brotherhood, about the Master and the life of the community, about the mountains where they used to spend the summer together, and about the sunrise that they welcomed every morning with songs and *paneurhythmy* – dance-like exercises created for that purpose. This is how I came to the Raspberry Garden.

The Raspberry Garden was an oasis in the middle of the city. The owner, whom my acquaintance married when they were both middle-aged, had been one of the major Bulgarian publishers before the communist coup. At the same time he was also an important person in the movement of the Brotherhood of Light. Before the war, he bought the rights to publish a philosophy series called "Immortal Thoughts" from an American publishing house. The series presented great philosophers from Confucius to Montaigne, Voltaire, and Rousseau. This man was persecuted by the communist government both because of his involvement with Dânov's movement and because he had published non-Marxist philosophy. His publishing house, as well as his home, were "confiscated." The two daughters he had from his first marriage had found refuge in the West. He was not allowed to have a job, nor to leave the country. The authorities had been trying to ruin his existence systematically since 1944. The Raspberry Garden was the only thing he had left from his previous life. In fact, selling raspberries and blackcurrant on a farmers' market was the only means he had to keep his head above water. Soon before I met him, the authorities had warned him that they would take away his Raspberry Garden too.

The Brotherhood of Light included people with different ethnic and religious backgrounds. It was an open association of people with no formal conditions whatsoever for entering or leaving it. There was no initiation ritual either. It represented no order and no sect but a way of thinking and of living. Before 1944 all the members of the community in Sofia lived together in the same neighborhood, as in a commune. This neighborhood was located in the outskirts east of the city. The members called it *Sunrise*. Atheistic Bulgaria did not tolerate any spiritual movements or religious sects though. Nevertheless, the government could not simply eradicate Dânov's movement. There were too many followers in Switzerland, France, California, and other places in the world. The discourses given by Dânov, written down in shorthand by disciples and published abroad, could be found in some of the major libraries around the world. To ban Dânov's teachings straight out would have attracted international attention. Thus, the regime decided to allow the existence of a limited number of registered members. Nevertheless, because of the specific philosophical platform of this school of thought and the international contacts of the community, the movement was considered "dangerous," and its followers spies and outright enemies of the state.

The regime had already virtually destroyed the brotherhood in the '50s. The property of the community, including Dânov's philosophical works, was confiscated. The brotherhood had never had any kind of a temple. Its sacred places were the meadows and the mountains. Thus, the authorities had to take apart the summer camp which the followers used to set up for many years in the Rila Mountain, near the area called the Seven Lakes. On and off over the years the campers had been asked to leave the area until by the early '70s the camp was strictly forbidden. The community hall where the members gathered for different events was demolished and people were no longer allowed to welcome the sunrise in the open with songs and *paneurhythmy* (the dance exercises).

Even though the brothers and sisters (as the members of the Brotherhood of Light called each other) lived together as if in a commune, they all had their private lives. Those who had saved some money before the war owned small houses in the Sunrise neighborhood. In the communist economic system private property did not exist but there was the so-called personal property that was related mostly to home ownership. Many people lost their houses or apartments after the coup of 1944 but others were allowed to keep a limited number of square meters as living space. In the beginning of the '70s the property of all homeowners in the Sunrise neighborhood was expropriated.

Bulgaria was very important to the Soviets for various strategic reasons. As a consequence, already since the '60s the size of the diplomatic corps in the country could be compared to that of an ethnic minority. The Soviet diplomats in Sofia had their own school, their own shops, and all they still needed was to have their own fortress. In *socialist planned economy* it was often the case that buildings or even entire settlements would be destroyed on the whims of some bureaucrats so that pompous figments of their fantasy or "edifices of the creation of a multilaterally developed socialist society" could be erected precisely in their stead. In the mid-'50s, for example, three villages were demolished when the gigantic water reservoir "Iskâr" was built near Sofia. Taking with them their meager possessions, the villagers migrated to the neighboring towns, where most of them were housed in basement rooms under inhuman conditions. When the Soviets announced that they wished to build a new embassy, the government suggested that they build it in the Sunrise neighborhood. The last followers of the Dânov movement, who were still living in that part of the city, were forcefully evicted from their homes and had no chance but to accept ridiculously inadequate financial compensations.

Despite these circumstances, my friend from the Raspberry Garden started building a new house on the small piece of land which was not going to belong to him much longer. He was building the house on his own – with his bare hands. "The fact that things are destroyed is no reason not to build them at all," he said.

The only place that still belonged to the brotherhood was the gravesite of the Master – a small garden, surrounded by poplar trees and cypresses. The flower beds were full of carefully selected plants and herbs, some of which were very rare. In the middle of the garden, there was an elliptical green area, framed by a low cast iron fence painted in white – perhaps less than half a meter tall. The disciples tended to the garden and if you didn't know that this was a gravesite, it would have never crossed your mind. The Brotherhood did not organize any memorial services or other events there. Every now and then the passers-by could see a woman or a man sitting quietly on one of the pretty white painted benches and they could only guess that these men and women wanted to pay reverence to their Master – as if in silent meditation. One year after the Soviets had started building the embassy a huge imposing stone wall was erected around the enormous space designated for this fortress – right across the Master's gravesite. At the time, the only difference between this wall and the Great Wall of China seemed to be that the Soviet wall in Sofia was not built over the course of many centuries. We never saw what was there behind the wall. However, all sorts of surveillance cameras were attached to the outside of the wall and some of them were meant to help observe the gravesite too.

In those days, almost only the followers of Dânov were vegetarians in Bulgaria. Vegetarians were generally despised and considered to be nuts. The only vegetarian restaurant in Sofia was closed for a long time as a preventive measure against possible mass meetings of followers of the movement. Mountain hut keepers were instructed to watch for vegetarians among their visitors. If they noticed any, they were supposed to report this to the closest state security office with no delay. It was a real conspiracy to eat cheese when one was trekking in the mountains.

From time to time there were also crisis raids accompanied by house searches and arrests. In the focus of those raids were usually two main topics. One was the dissemination of Dânov's incriminated books and lectures, as the followers called them. The other one was transferring the Master's remains, something that would have meant to the followers to lose the only sacred place that belonged to all of them together. Legend has it that the freemasons had their representatives amongst the governments of different countries. Unlike them, the disciples of Dânov did not have a single person in the communist Bulgarian government. Thus, they had to be constantly on the alert. For some reason or another, however, destroying this particular movement turned out to be too difficult, even for the communist regime.

...

The communists feared most of all people who were tolerant in their way of thinking. They needed puppets whose heads could be stuffed with pre-prepared models in order to be able to manipulate them better. The safest method to control people's intellectual life was, as they thought, to reject every single phenomenon that strayed from the dogma. Our society was full of disavowed outsiders, but it was unthinkable that organized groups of dissidents might appear. The regime was trying to break down any uncommon type of association – by using all possible sorts of "games." To do this, players were needed too. Most of all young players.

It wasn't difficult to figure out whether someone was connected to the Brotherhood of Light. It was known that I was a "grass eater," as they used to call vegetarians, and also that I was often trekking in the mountains. On top of it, I was friends with a well-known member of the brotherhood, the man from the Raspberry Garden, who was considered a dangerous opponent of the regime. Worse! I was not a member of the Komsomol, the youth organization of the communist party.

Everywhere One Goes

I believe that in those days there was not another single living soul between the ages of fourteen and thirty that was not a member of the Komsomol. The fact that I was not a member was actually due to an accident. At the time in question, there were only two Jews in the Music High School – George and me. George came from France. As a young teenager he had had problems with the French police because he was involved in some street fights, and his father, a left-wing Jew, decided to send him to relatives in Bulgaria, hoping that the fiery character of his boy would be curbed more easily in a communist society. High school students were accepted in the Komsomol automatically, usually in the eighth grade. When the time to accept our classmates came, George and I were told that we would be accepted at a later point, together with another age group, because we were born too late in the given year. This happened in 1967, the year the Six Day War raged in the Middle East. Following the example of the Soviets, Bulgaria interrupted its diplomatic relations with Israel. This was the beginning of a long campaign against Israel and against Zionism. No one in the country knew what Zionism actually meant. However, there were three particular definitions in Bulgaria that equaled life sentence: to be considered a capitalist, a revisionist, or a Zionist. Apparently, my French classmate and I were considered potential Zionists. In the same year I decided to apply for a permission to complete my high school education as a private student. My reasons were unrelated to politics, but when my application was approved, I realized that in this way I could avoid many political problems too. This is how I remained outside the circles of reliable organized youth.

Sometime later the authorities were shocked to discover that I was independent – from school as well as from the Komsomol. According to the constitution joining the youth organization should have been a voluntary act, but in reality, this was as voluntary as the so-called *manifestations* or parades on official holidays. The options were either to be nice and quiet and march in your row, together with everyone else, or to expect various kinds of "sanctions." As it turned out, since I was a private student and thus did not belong to the Komsomol organization in my school, I had to join the organization in my neighborhood. I was told that it was only by mistake that I had not been accepted in the Komsomol much earlier, and that there was no way I could graduate from high school without having this membership. I consciously wanted to stay away from this organization, but at the same time I was absolutely convinced that the Komsomol existed only on paper, in order to keep a bunch of functionaries busy. I believed that this membership was just a formality and tried not to oppose it.

I started paying my membership contributions to the organization in the neighborhood on a regular basis. However, I was asked to take an entry exam. Usually, the preparation for this exam consisted simply of memorizing the statute and the program of the organization, but since I was considered a "special case" I was confronted with a different approach. The secretary of the local city district Komsomol organization started paying me occasional unexpected home visits. She wanted to learn more about my family relationships, to see who I socialized with, what time I got up in the morning, and what I liked to eat. I had to report to her about everything I was doing, and I had the feeling that she was poking deep in my stomach with a long rusty needle.

Among other suspicious things, the secretary had noticed a few forbidden books in my room, including the Bible and books with Dânov's lectures. One day she announced that, as an entry exam, I had to give a presentation on atheism.

"I really have no time for this," I said, trying to get out of the situation.

She insisted: "When?"

"I can't write well."

"But you write poetry and short stories."

"Even so, I really don't want to give a talk on this topic."

"You have to convince the organization that you are not simply paying your contribution, but that you were fully conscious of what you were doing when you joined. Only then would your membership be valid. And by the way, why do you have a problem with atheism?"

What now?

Did they want to re-educate me or to expose me? What was the real goal behind this request? How was I to master the situation?

And then I had a thought. I could use the opportunity to talk to other young people about things that they certainly had never heard about before.

I wrote my presentation. I focused on a historical overview of the foundation of the Bulgarian Orthodox Church and different religious movements in the country. I went over the biography of Petâr Dânov in detail and tried to explain briefly the ideas of his school of thought. My goal was to offer as much information as possible. When I actually gave my presentation, however, I was asked how I personally saw all the questions I discussed. I wanted to avoid answering directly, so I explained that if we wanted to promote atheism, we should first make sure that we had very good knowledge of the philosophical schools and theories we wanted to contradict. I also said that I could say neither Yes nor No to things I was not familiar with. My conscience was clear, but from that day on I was considered to be an "apolitical parasite" – a description that, under the communists, was almost worse than to be "dangerous." A few months after I gave my presentation, I received a phone call at home. It was someone from the State Security. He was calling unofficially, he said. I had to appear in front of the authorities, and I was supposed to keep this secret. Naturally, I told my father right away. He thought for a while and decided that we should not play with fire, that I had no reason to worry, and that I should go.

. . .

I showed up in the State Security office. For the first time. I was nineteen. Two agents were waiting for me. One of them was offensive and hot tempered and the other a bit more balanced and polite. I realized only later that this was quite a common method of interrogation. One of them had to throw me off balance and the other was supposed to calm me down. The expected result was that I would be so confused that, eventually, I would come out with the "truth."

"Why do you think did we order you to come here?"

I bit the bait and started telling them about the German professor whom I met in Belgrade and some other contacts I had abroad, about the embassy of West Germany and the books I received as a gift.

"Don't you see that with or without the stipend you are already enticed in the net of the capitalist enemies? And what kind of people are you surrounded with in the first place? Only parasites, strangers from the West, divorced people, and sect members whom you address with *Madam* and *Sir* rather than with *Comrade*! How low do you want to fall?"

I did not want to let them scare me but I was quite shaken. They were talking about things I could never deny and about people I did not want to hurt. I had to be completely on my guard. I got a cramp in my left arm and my right hand was trembling but at that point, my convictions prevailed – once and for all.

I denied any attempt on the part of my friend from the Raspberry Garden to convert me and make me a member of the "sect" or to talk me into any kind of an attitude, hostile to the state. Regardless, the agents threatened that if I did not break up this contact immediately there would be consequences. The alternative was to spy on my friends and, if I noticed "*something,*" to report to the State Security. Eventually, I had to put on paper everything I had said – as I remembered it. They gave me paper – blank white sheets of paper. I was not allowed to sign my piece of writing.

The news about this interrogation did not surprise my friends from the *Brotherhood of Light*. They were used to things like that. I myself, however, had to live for the next seventeen years terribly frustrated and in constant fear that I might say or do something wrong, something that could harm either myself or the people around me.

Otherwise, I kept visiting the Raspberry Garden as before and continued reading books about different teachings and religions. Every now and then, for the sake of my safety and the safety of my family and friends, I had to let the incriminated literature disappear from my home. When the air was clear, my books came back to me again and we continued our coexistence.

Fahrenheit 451

This is exactly how *Doctor Zhivago, One Day in the Life of Ivan Denisovich, The First Circle*, *Cancer Ward*, and many other books wandered through the streets. Often in the evening, one could see wandering books in a hurry, hidden in overcoat pockets and carried by young and old. Whoever wanted to read them had to hurry to get rid of them again because they could betray you.

One day, through my boyfriend, I became acquainted with a ghost-collection of books like that. These books were no longer wandering. They rested comfortably on the shelf and felt safe and self-assured. They were at peace thanks to the experience of suffering. Like their owner, Duke M., the son of a Russian noble family, had left Russia with the Whites after the Civil War. He had worked in Bulgaria as a scholar in the National Library. Now, he was sitting in his rocking chair, calm and relaxed, and he smiled. He was involved in the trial of the disseminators of Solzhenitsyn's books, which was held behind closed doors. Bulgaria had to mimic the Soviet campaign against Solzhenitsyn which followed his Nobel Prize award in 1970. Several people who were trying to smuggle Solzhenitsyn's books into Bulgaria from Eastern and from Western countries were caught at customs. A trial against them was immediately organized. Naturally, there was nothing about it in the press. Those who were involved in the trial were afraid to talk. Nevertheless, a few details slipped out. We learned that some people were brought to the trial as defendants and others only as witnesses. What *witnesses* meant in this case, though, was remarkable because the trial had consequences not only for the accused but also for the witnesses. The Duke was only a witness. He had in his possession all of Solzhenitsyn's books, which he had most likely received from his daughters who lived in Switzerland. Once, he had even lent one of these books to a friend. The regime considered this act "dissemination of incriminated literature." After the trial, Duke M.'s pension was stopped and he was allowed to work only as a porter, loading and unloading trucks. He was seventy-two. As a consequence, he suffered untreatable back pain. He knew that he would never be permitted to visit his two daughters in Switzerland, and he was at peace. He had nothing more to lose other than his smile and his brilliant intellect. Once in a while the government took away from him one book or another, but he was able to get over this too.

. . .

There were also authors who wandered around with their never-published works. One day I met one of those poets in the mountains. We had lost our way in a deep-winter-wood. The pine trees, heavy with snow, were sweating under the March sun. There was no trail in sight and the rocks around portended solitude. Up there, in a timeless endless space, we were three of us – a young poet, an artist, and I. We spoke in verses and colors. We were writing and painting our friendship.

The young poet had failed in the world down below. In the beginning of the '70s, he had founded a disco-club. Sometimes he would read his poems to the members of the club. One of those members reported him to the Security, and after that he knew that he was under surveillance. One day he decided to establish some rules regarding the club membership in the form of written articles. The state accused him of founding an illegal organization. At the time, the existence of any organized group of people that was not under the direct control of the communist party was unthinkable. If more than five people got together two times in a row, even if they would simply have a cup of coffee, this would raise suspicions in neighbors, in the party organization, and eventually in the government. Consequently, the club of my acquaintance was closed. All works of this poet were confiscated during a house raid. After all this happened, the young man tried several times to go to Paris, hoping that he could publish something there. After his third attempt the authorities explained to him very convincingly that he would never see Paris, particularly because he was a good poet. Finally, he understood. That day, when we were lost in the mountains, he said that one could fight for and win real freedom only in oneself. He no longer cared whether they would let him travel to Paris or not, for Paris was in him and no one could ever take it away.

Of course, some people did care about going to Paris.

. . .

Once upon a time there was a little girl. She started writing poems and short stories when she was nine. A young established writer became her writing confidant and kept advising her over many years.

After he had graduated from the university, he had to do his mandatory military service. Most of his superiors in the army despised and hated him because he was an intellectual – fine and gentle, with a pale countenance, and long thin fingers. His sergeant, a short stocky guy with a potbelly, full of inferiority complexes, must have decided to avenge himself on the young soldier, and he tortured him as well as he could. Eventually, the sergeant sent the young soldier to work, day and night, at a water pump – his legs, up to the knees, in cold sludge. Until the young man ended in a hospital. He was sent back to his unit as *fit for service with restrictions.* The next day he was standing at the water pump again. Until his service time ended. This man, one of the best Bulgarian writers of his generation, walks on crutches to this day, for he has an incurable bone disease.

What happened to her friend in the military filled the young girl with consternation and she wrote a short story about him – about the way the military crippled young men physically and psychologically. This was her best story till then. As usual, she wanted to show it to her friend. At that point, he was editor in one of the major literary journals. He was sitting in a comfortable armchair, in the middle of a spacious room, full of light. He read and read. Then he got up from the armchair, took his crutches, limped slowly toward the girl, put his arm around her shoulders, and said:

"If you want me to keep helping you write, then you should forget that things like this happen. You should never write again about the army or the police. Forget about them! You wrote a good story, but the action should play somewhere else."

The girl went home, put the manuscript of her story in a drawer, and thought that she would never write again. That country was full of dead corpses of wishes and ideas. It was like a catacomb of dying hopes and initiatives.

Midas 2000[6]

Fifteen years passed before I had my second encounter with the State Security. I was already married, had two children, a wonderful job, and I was still following my dreams. My first husband came from an intelligent, educated, Christian-Orthodox family. At the time, people in Bulgaria used two distinct terms for the differences in social status – *our guys* and *the former ones*. *Our guys* were all of those who subscribed to the ideological system or who clearly wanted to adjust to it. To count as a *former one* was extremely inconvenient. This was a description for people who had either been rich in the past or had owned a business, or for those who were educated in Western Europe. The views of such people were considered at the very best to be *unstable* and *susceptible* to Western influence. Generally, they were seen as enemies of the regime. My first husband's parents had graduated from the American College in Sofia before the war. His mother was an English teacher. She was a real admirer of Anglo-Saxon culture and her biggest dream was that someday one of her children or grandchildren would be educated in America. The father completed a doctorate degree in Amsterdam and audited courses in Oxford as well. My husband was quite knowledgeable in history and politics. He listened regularly to the BBC, the Voice of America, and Radio Free Europe – as long as their broadcasts were not jammed. He also kept in touch with a classmate of his, who had escaped through the border in a very risky way and lived at the time in Washington D.C. Already as a very young man my husband was clearly against the communist regime. He shared my views and, like me, wished to leave Bulgaria. We thought about many different possibilities for carrying out this plan. We were only waiting for the right time to come.

...

In 1986 my uncle in Israel became very ill. He had no children and he loved me very much. He realized that his life was coming to its end and he really

6 In Greco-Roman mythology Midas is a king of Phrygia, known for his greed. When Dionysus wanted to reward Midas for having found his wandering companion, the satyr Silenus, the king wished that everything he touched would turn to gold. He realized his foolishness only when his food turned to gold and he nearly starved to death.

wanted to see me one more time. In addition, his wife was getting old and she could no longer take care of him alone. My uncle called me and asked if I could go to Israel. I agreed. He sent me an invitation, in which he was asking the authorities to speed up issuing my travel permission, explaining that he was on his death bed and that he needed my help.

I submitted my first application for a permit to travel to the West, hoping that I would not have any problems because I was married and the mother of two children. To the authorities this usually would have meant that someone I would never abandon would remain in the country as a pawn. A whole month passed by. Meanwhile I was calling my uncle every other day, nevertheless he began to doubt that I really wanted to go to him. Then I received the answer. No.

How should I describe my reaction? Suddenly I was sentenced. Being innocent. Without a trial. Without an explanation. Forever. For the first answer was always the most important one. If once you had a "no" in your file, marked in red, you were branded. Finished.

I was walking around the city and did not know where my head was. The buildings seemed to be getting bigger and bigger and the streets smaller and smaller. As if the buildings were going to collapse on top of me. I was in a gigantic cage and I was seeing grids all around. I thought I was going mad. The most painful question was "Why?" What crime did I commit? How was I dangerous? Or was this punishment? What for?

I had to keep a clear head and to act. First, I went to the office hours of the Chief of the Passport Department in the Ministry of the Interior. I walked into that building unsure of myself and completely cramped. At the door stood a militia man. I asked to register for a meeting. He asked why I was there. We started a wretched conversation. I tried to explain that my travel application was rejected and that I wanted to speak to the chief about it.

Why go to Israel? Because I wanted to visit my uncle. Was I Jewish? Fifty-fifty. So, what was I? Just me. What did my uncle want? He was sick. What was the matter? He was dying. Why did I have to go to him? Because he had no children and wanted to see me. Aha! So, I was going to inherit everything!

Everyone, from the doorman to the biggest fish, who eventually gave me the travel permit, was concerned with the question whether I would inherit something. At that point I was not yet aware of the fact that if one received inheritance abroad, the lion's share would fall into the hands of the state. I learned how exactly this worked many years later from a rich Bulgarian in Germany. Not only through huge taxes. The government was forcing heirs to give what they called "donations" to the state, to different organizations, to Bulgarian embassies abroad, and even to prominent persons. An heir could lay claim to his/her inheritance only after all necessary documents for the donation were already signed. Frequently, people were presented with documents in a foreign language so that they did not even know what they were signing. My uncle was the director of a bank and I was able to play off this fact quite well against the greed of the authorities.

Even so, after the Chief of the passport department said to me "We shall see… " I realized that I should explore other options. First, I asked my mother to turn for help to her former connections. Her position, however, was difficult.

…

My mother!

My mother was both a victim and a typical example of the psychic perversions the system caused. Before the war her father had been an actor and administrator of the National Theater. Consequently, he moved in the prominent social circles of the pre-war times and even knew Tsar Boris III personally. After the coup of 1944 some communist noticed the portrait of the Tsar hanging on the wall in my grandfather's office. My grandfather was arrested for no clear reason and kept for a short while in prison. That meant the end of his career in the theater.

My mother had been accepted as a student at the Art Academy in Sofia in 1943, just before the end of the war. The queen visited this beginning class for some particular event. There were photos taken at the formal reception. The queen recognized my mother and shook her hand. There was a photo taken of this. In 1944 the secretary of the Komsomol organization wanted my mother to be expelled from the academy, because she "had contacts with the king's family and had a bourgeois face herself." However, classmates of hers, who knew her well from secondary school, were able to come to her rescue. Nevertheless, my mother always had problems because of her heritage.

Now she had two daughters. She loved them more than anything. She was obsessed with them. She was an unhappy woman who had once had many dreams. Not a single one of them had been fulfilled. No matter what the cost, she would not allow life to pass by her children in the same unremarkable way as it was passing by her. She was well aware of the way one had to live when excluded from society and she wanted for her daughters to adjust to that society. Without realizing it, she became a conformist because of her wish to see her children succeed. That wish was like an addiction.

When my mother realized that I was in trouble with the authorities because of the Dânov movement, she wanted me to stay away from those friendships. We spent many years in fights and disagreements until we totally lost real connection with each other. But she fought and fought – for me, and for my future. She complained about my involvement with the movement to everyone. She even asked her "Connection" for help. The only consequence of that was that all the information she gave to the "Connection" was forwarded to the State Security. Whatever I tried to deny at different points was pointless, the State Security had a reliable source of the truth – my mother.

When my application for a travel permit was rejected in 1986 and I had to ask my mother for help, she did not know what to do. She had personally told her "Connection" things about me that one could not easily forget, including the fact that I would probably want to escape. Thus, we could forget about that key person. Another acquaintance of my mother, however, came up with the idea that, most likely, I would receive an inheritance in Israel. She thought that the state might be interested in this fact and offered to help. One day, a man called me and proposed in a very secretive way that we meet in a café. He did not give me his name, nor did he say what institution he was working for.

I went to the café. A nice young man was waiting for me. He introduced himself only with his given name. We had a long conversation about me and my family. Then he asked if I had contacts to members of "Dânov's sect" abroad. Apparently, the authorities were always on the alert, expecting an international Dânov's sect plot. In fact, after the owner of the Raspberry Garden had died, I no longer had contacts to the movement. The fact that I did not belong to the "international conspiracy of Dânov's followers" seemed to be very comforting. Briefly, the man was ready to put in a word on my behalf, but under two conditions. In the first place, I was not supposed to talk to anyone about our meeting, and in the second–there was a catch in this whole thing. Upon my return, I was supposed to report in writing about all the places I had been to, all the people I had talked to, and also what the conversations were about. This was it. Report about what, I asked. Just in general. I had to make a decision very quickly. If I said NO, I was probably going to miss the last chance I could get. If I said YES... Would I then become a player in the game? I knew that I was actually going to a funeral and that I was going to spend most of the time at home with my aunt. I was neither a hero nor a revolutionary. I had no ideas for which I was ready to die. I had only ideas for which I wanted to live. I agreed. However, I warned the man very clearly that I was not willing to cooperate with the Security. I also told him that I would have never agreed if I were not certain that I was actually going to say goodbye to my dying uncle and I would not be doing much else. The man asked if my uncle was planning to leave me some inheritance. I thought it was possible, but I wasn't sure. Two days later I received my first passport. When I went through the border passport checking at the airport, I had the feeling that I had conquered the entire world. Through a lousy piece of paper.

Shalom

After a long wait in Athens, the El-Al plane finally arrived. Passengers were called up and we all got on the bus to the plane. It was the beginning of August. Summer heat in Athens. Everybody was wearing light summer clothes. In the past, I had had this inferiority complex that my skin is very ugly – white as chalk and covered with freckles. I was afraid to wear a dress with a décolleté and I always had to mind the sun. I simply looked different from everybody else. That day, when I was standing in the bus to the El-Al airplane I suddenly noticed the arm of a woman next to me. Her skin was pale. With freckles. I looked up to her neck. She had freckles everywhere. The man next to her too. And the little girl there in the corner. And the two boys. A bus full of freckles. People like me. I looked exactly like them. I was not different. My skin did not call any attention. It was fascinating. I think I have never felt as Jewish as at that particular moment. This was the enchanting fascination with belonging – the fascination with belonging of a misfit. I was happy.

I had no particular image of Israel. The West, which to the authorities meant all non-socialist countries and included particularly the "Zionist" state of Israel, was taboo for the Bulgarian media. I had only a few random pictures in my head: small streets where one could be shot unexpectedly, old Hebrew cave tombs, and Thomas Mann's descriptions in the Joseph tetralogy. When my aunt picked me up from the airport and we drove to the hospital where my uncle was, I was surprised to see that there were completely normal houses and streets. What did I expect? That buildings would have the shape of pyramids or the streets would go over the roofs?

My uncle was still able to recognize me. He asked why I came so late. He died three hours after my arrival. In my hands. The funeral was on the next day. I hated the Bulgarian authorities, I hated the System, I hated the world in which my basic rights as a human being were denied to me.

I spent forty days in Israel. I got to see the country in a remarkable way.

According to Jewish tradition, it is customary that when someone dies, the family stays at home and mourns the deceased for a week. At the same time, friends and acquaintances are supposed to keep the mourning family company and to take care of them. During this Hevel-week my aunt and

I were sitting at home and we were visited by dozens of people from all around the country. Each one of them brought a little piece of Israel along. These people told me stories about the founding of the state and the pioneer times, about the different countries they came from, about the death camps and the war. It was as if a whole world had come to me. Seven days later, when I was first allowed to leave the house, I had the feeling that I had lived in Israel for years. I was expecting to see exactly what I did see. The only real surprise was the sunset in the Mediterranean. A friend brought me to the *Tayelet*, the Promenade in Tel Aviv, for my first long walk. We were walking barefoot through the lukewarm water along the coast. Suddenly I realized that the sky was crimson red and the sun was half way sunk behind the green horizon. The sunrise and the sunset have always meant a lot to me. However, I was used to seeing the sun rise over the Black Sea and now I was spellbound by this fire sinking into the sea. How different the world could look! How limited and relative my images of it!

...

The most impressive experience was Jerusalem. I visited Jerusalem several times. The first time my aunt and I went on a pilgrimage to the Holy Sepulcher. I walked along Via Dolorosa and up to the Church of the Holy Sepulcher. I went also to the Wailing Wall and left a small note in between the ancient stones, as was customary. But all this was simply a tourist sightseeing. I was particularly disappointed by the Holy Sepulcher. Since my aunt was a Christian, she wanted to go there. It sounded fascinating. When we arrived there, we had to wait about forty minutes in a queue before our turn came. Then, at the door to the church, someone tried to sell us a pilgrim certificate of a hundred dollars. We refused and walked in. After another half hour I was already standing under the stone vault at the entrance to the small space where the Holy Sepulcher was. A guard who was standing at the threshold stuck a small candle into my hand, demanded five dollars, and whispered into my ear: “Please move on quickly.” The crowd was pushing me forward and I was outside only a few seconds later. At the shuk, the market in front of the church, Arabs, Jews, and Christians were selling kitschy souvenirs as relics. Out of the blue, a devout nun from who knows what order grabbed my aunt by the hand and wanted to show her the “real” sepulcher of Jesus.

The second time I was in Jerusalem for a few days, together with a man who was born to be a guide through this city. To me, Jerusalem was the cradle of my heritage. Like the roots of the millennia old olive trees in the Garden Gat Shmanim[7]. Like the stones in the Temple of King David and the Wailing Wall. With every cell of my body I felt how, coming from the past, I represented a thin thread to the future. I was looking at the cave tombs around the fringes of the city and I was thinking that somewhere there, under the desert rocks, must rest my own ancestors. I was nothing but something that has always existed. Here, on this earth, for thousands of years, for eternity. Like the elements. To touch a stone from ancient ruins, to lean on the trunk of an age-old tree, to be able to feel the firm connection to past times somewhere in our life, and then to take responsibility for the future – this was Jerusalem to me, to be one with the unchanging.

In addition to mystical experience, Jerusalem brought me also a very special friend. This was a friendship like the one between Don Carlos and Marquis De Posa, a closeness like the one in the Chorus of the Hebrew Slaves from Nabucco. It was one of those relationships that one could believe have begun millions of years ago. This was the person with whom for the very first time I dared to discuss my plan to escape. Given his extraordinary sensibility I did not have to explain much. Each word we exchanged was meaningful and remained imprinted in my memory, probably forever.

Today, when I look back at those days, everything appears to have been so well planned that I must simply laugh at my desperation or at my hesitation to make decisions. I know, however, that all that was natural, for we can never see things from the perspective of the future. Sometimes we try to break through a wall with our head while next to us there is an open door which we have not noticed yet. Perhaps this is a better way of learning, and I still had to learn a lot.

After many considerations and emotions, I decided to go back to Bulgaria. I was torn apart. On one hand, it was very possible that this had been my only chance to emigrate. I received my passport with so much trouble that I could not know then if this could ever happen again. On the

---

7 Gethsemane

other hand, my children were there, and it did not seem very probable that they would be somehow able to join me. I even consulted the Sochnut, the Jewish Agency for Israel. Until today I can hear the soft voice of the gray-haired gentleman with whom I talked about this. He did not let me fool myself. At the time, Bulgaria had no diplomatic relations with Israel. Consequently, there was no formal way to apply for a family reunion. After we discussed the situation for a while, this gentleman said to me that, if he was judging me correctly, I would not survive for long without my children. He discouraged me from immigrating to Israel at this particular moment in very clear words. Like many other people, back then I saw things only from the perspective of a snail. On my back, I was carrying my little shell of political views and it could not cross my mind that three years later the borders of the Socialist Bloc would be open, and the new migration of peoples would begin. I thought that it was over with my dreams and hopes. At night I could not sleep at all and I was constantly trying to imagine both alternatives. This was an old technique. I learned this method in the Raspberry Garden. When we have to make a difficult decision, we should try to imagine all possibilities in detail. The right decision would be the one that brings us to a completely harmonious state of mind. We should feel peace and satisfaction. We should feel no tension, no distress that might be coming from a dissonance. This is a beautiful thing. Given you are aware of what you feel. At the time, that trick did not work. I was totally confused. Everything in my head was spinning into a muddle. In order to be back with my children again I had to give up my biggest dream. It was even worse. That dream was already in my grasp. I had to give up either the reality of a dream or the dream of another reality. To let it drop from the palm of my hand. But to turn that dream into reality I had to give up my children. At least for a while. I do not think that there is anything more horrible that could be taken away from a person – the dream of one's life, or one's children.

Until my last day in Israel I hesitated and thought that maybe I should stay in Israel after all. Until the last night, the last hour, and the last minute. I hesitated still at the border control, and I hesitated during the stopover at the airport in Athens. But I could not stop thinking of my children in the first place.

In Athens I missed the plane to Sofia by accident. I had to wait another twelve hours, until the next morning. I wanted to go outside the airport. It was impossible. The Greeks would not let any Bulgarian out of the transit area, unless they had a visa. I realized that I was locked up again and that I had probably made the biggest sacrifice in my life.

A sacrifice makes a person grow. When we part with people or things to which we are attached we suffer because we cannot accept the loss. Instead of diminishing the distance by focusing on the person or the place we have parted with we focus on the very distance and, by doing that, we increase it. Everything I had to give up, in order to be with my children again, was in me, and I knew that from that point on no one could ever take anything away from me. As the young poet in the mountains once said: "Paris was in me."

Eye for an Eye

When I returned it was very difficult for me to readjust to my everyday life. Here, in the West, when we travel, we may not see such drastic contrasts between one Western country and another. To return from abroad to Bulgaria was for everyone who experienced this a real shock. Despite all the love toward our family, our friends, and everything that is close to us at home. The fact that we were compelled to remain in this country, that we were forcefully imprisoned, pushed many of us so far away from it that often we did not even realize what we would miss if we left it. It took me a long time to get used again to the careful conversations, to the petty daily problems, to people's envy of my travels outside the Iron Curtain, to being spied on, to the fear in which we all lived, and to the ignorance and the alienation caused by the isolation of our society from the rest of the world. On top of this, it appeared that I had a new personal problem.

Before, I was considered half Jewish. This allowed friends and acquaintances who had something against my Semitic origin to relate simply to my other half. However, in Bulgaria, to have been in Israel meant much more than to be just Jewish. To many Bulgarians that meant to be a Zionist. People assumed that since I had visited Israel, I must feel more Jewish and must be more committed to my heritage than I was before. The fact alone that one had visited Israel meant a YES to Judaism and to the Jewish State. Consequently, one was considered also a potential enemy of the Bulgarian state. In the almost two decades after the six-day-war, Bulgaria had consistently supported the Arabic states which were against Israel. Bulgaria delivered weapons to them, trained Arabic terrorists, and sent specialists to the Arabic countries. We offered all sorts of diplomatic, economic, medical, and other help. Otherwise, Bulgarian Jews were generally not considered to be dangerous. Most of them were old communists, comrades from the time of the partisan fights and the socialist coup. The majority of them had participated in the fight against fascism out of a deep and honest conviction. When I was young, the institutionalized Center of Jewish Culture developed as an outpost for systematic propaganda against the state of Israel.

The publishers of the single Jewish newspaper, *Evreiski Vesti* [Jewish News), had sold their souls to the devil and had forged a pact with the communist regime. This newspaper was always the first to condemn the military and political decisions Israel made. More importantly, it was the platform for the distribution of slanders concerning the country of Israel. The Center of Jewish Culture organized "renovations" of the synagogue for years, so that no service could be held there any longer. The celebrations of any holidays that were quite common when I was a little child, were forbidden, and the club where one could have gefilte fish on Shabbat was closed. Gradually, the entire life of the community was extinguished. The old rabbi died and his son, who was a mediocre party journalist, took over the diminished Jewish flock in Sofia.

In Sofia, funerals remained the only occasions where one could meet large numbers of Jews and take some advantage of the services offered by the Center – a continuously repeated burial of Jewishness. Several times a year, when someone among the Jews who was not a communist died the rabbi had to take care of them. In addition to family and friends, other members of the community went to those funerals too, for there always had to be at least twelve men at the funeral so that prayers from the Torah could be read.

The Jewish cemetery remained the only place where one could meet people he knew in the past and learn what had happened to them in the meantime, who had married, and in which family there had been a child born. There people talked for hours about the past, about the war, about the labor camps in Bulgaria, and about the time after. Most of my impressions of the living Jewry in Bulgaria were cemetery impressions. A mourning procession of a millennia-long experience.

...

Despite the political barriers though, many Israelis of Bulgarian heritage came to Bulgaria on holiday. In fact, these were the only foreigners to whom one could more easily have some contact. There was no language problem and most of these Israelis stayed with family, including in our neighborhood. Usually, they were well positioned in society and generous, which to many meant rich. Thus, over the course of the years, Bulgarians developed a certain envy toward Israelis, which resulted in categorizing them as "rich and dangerous." This is what the allegedly non-existent anti-Semitism in Bulgaria looked like in the last twenty years of communism.

Now, coming back from Israel, I was personally exposed to this attitude, in every possible respect.

The first shock I had was caused by the way I was received by my neighbors after I returned from Israel. By that time, I had already lived in this apartment building for about four years. In Bulgaria, the relationships we had with our neighbors were an important part of our lives. It was particularly important for people who lived in new developments in the periphery of the city to get along really well. These neighborhoods were a bit remote, without a phone connection and with pretty bad public transportation. Thus, people had to count on each other. Children had to get up at five in the morning and to wait a very long time for the public bus to go to school (school buses were a rarity). We all were often looking for someone to take the children by car to school or, in the case of an emergency, to the doctor. In the same way, people needed each other when they had to repair something or to renovate their homes. Services were so expensive that we could rarely afford to hire a technician or an auto mechanic. Painting walls, putting in tiles, or repairing one's car was usually a common neighborly effort. It was also difficult to go to a concert or to the theater in the evening, particularly for those of us who had small children, and we had only one or maybe two state run TV programs. Instead, we were trying to compensate the lack of entertainment partly by socializing with our neighbors. Often, depending on age and interests, we developed deep emotional relations to our neighbors. We simply lived together, in a real community. There was, however, one negative side of this. Frequently, the men would get together over a glass of beer, wine, or brandy right after work and spend the whole evening drinking. That did not necessarily mean that all these men were drunkards but sometimes this lifestyle did lead to a socially determined alcoholism.

When I came back from Israel, I was received by the people with whom I had lived already for so long in very different ways. To some, my trip to Israel was like a myth, and they were anxious to hear how it was to be abroad. Others were interested to know only if I had become rich through the death of my uncle and what I had bought myself in the West (a term that had nothing to do with the four cardinal directions). There were also some who considered themselves really gracious that they continued seeing me. They excused maintaining their relationship to me with the fact that, although exposed to revisionism and Zionism, I was still half Bulgarian. This, apparently, made it worth forgiving me. But there were also people who were too afraid that their friendship with me could hurt them, and they gave it up. In any event, it was as if I was no longer the same person. Between me and many of my neighbors there was now a distance that could no longer be overcome.

...

Two days after my return the man from the State Security, thanks to whom I got my passport, called on me. He wanted to meet quasi-privately in a café. I had brought a small present for him, hoping that this would be enough as an expression of my gratitude. However, he reminded me very politely but also very clearly of our agreement. I had to write a report. I tried to explain that, in Israel, I had been only among relatives and that there was nothing special to tell, but he insisted and stressed that if I had any doubts, I should have thought about this before I left Bulgaria. The problem, though, was much more complicated than anything I could have imagined before I left.

Among the mourning guests I met in Israel was a friend of my uncle who was seen by the Bulgarian government as a very important political figure. He was a historian, a former member of the Central Committee of the communist party and agent in the State Security. As a dropout he was later persecuted. At that point, he was contributing pieces to the BBC, the Voice of America, and Radio Free Europe. His broadcasts on history and politics were well known. He also wrote the preface to the book by the Bulgarian author Georgi Markov, who was killed in London as a way of executing his Bulgarian death sentence in absentia. This turned my uncle's friend into a first rank state enemy. In short, he was a legend. I was very surprised to meet him in Israel because he wasn't Jewish. His wife, however, was. She was also a famous hero from the time of the partisan fights. When we met, we all realized that we liked each other. We saw each other several times. They even invited me to spend a few days in their home. These were a few wonderful days. We had long and interesting conversations. One could learn so much from these two people. They were highly intelligent, and they had been through unbelievable experiences. I even shared with them my plan to escape. When I decided, however, to return to Bulgaria, I told them about my agreement with the man from the State Security and asked them what they thought I should do, if this man wanted me to tell him about them.

"It would be better if you didn't go back," said the husband. "But if you decide to return, you certainly should not try to hide our acquaintance, for it is possible that the secret service already knows about it. If you try to lie you would look much more suspicious. Just the opposite. You should not ascribe any particular importance to our acquaintance."

When the man from the State Security started insisting that I write a report, I got scared. No matter what story I would have told him about this famous historian, the fact alone that I had met him would have been suspicious enough. So, I told the man that I would write a very general statement about my trip but that I had met someone in Israel with whom I did not wish the authorities to associate me. That line did not help. He wanted to have a detailed report. For the second time in my life my integrity was tested in such a particular way. To refuse could have meant for me and my family to have to take consequences on an unpredictable scale. At the same time, I could have easily endangered the lives of the two people I met in Israel through some innocent but unconsidered statement and I knew that the historian was sentenced to death in absentia for high treason. I was in deep trouble and did not try to pretend that I was not. Regardless of how I looked at the situation, it was impossible to avoid the danger and the conflict of conscience.

Meanwhile, the university where I was working as a German language instructor informed me that my part time contract would not be extended for the coming academic year. I suspected some connection between this decision and the report I was supposed to write for the State Security. I was never able to figure out if that was really the case, but many people were harassed in similar ways. The fact remains that two days after I submitted my report I was offered a job teaching at the university twenty-four hours per week, as usual.

I wrote a meaningless report about my stay in Israel spent among relatives and friends of my family. I did not mention any single surname, explaining that there is no formal address form in Ivrit[8] and people address each other only by their given names. Regarding the common attitude toward Bulgaria I did not have to lie. Bulgarian Jews liked Bulgaria. However, it was much more difficult to write the part of the report which concerned that particular political personality. The State Security was not satisfied with my first version. It was too general. They wanted to know his address, phone number, a description of the location of his apartment, and details about his character and his habits. I insisted that I did not know his phone number because I never called them. Since all street signs were written in Ivrit and I could not read this alphabet, I was able to argue that I did not know any of the street names. I also wrote that this man was very careful in front of me and did not want to get into any kind of a political discussion. In order to add some sense of detail to my report, I mentioned that we talked about the Bulgarian Tsar in exile.

I felt no guilt. My acquaintances in Israel knew that I was not going to deny the fact that we met if I was asked by the Bulgarian authorities, and, therefore, I had not acted behind their backs. My report was totally useless to the secret service, because there was nothing concrete in it. Nevertheless, this whole story got to me. At the time, there was always a lurking danger that the compromises one made with one's own conscience might be underestimated. All of a sudden, consciously or unconsciously, one could end up being enticed into the game and turn into a servant of the system. Personally, I did not want to let this happen to me. No matter what the cost.

I was never invited to the office of the State Security agent in charge of Israel. However, he was frequently quoted by his colleague to whom I had given my report "unofficially," and with whom I had to keep in touch. He used to call me every other month to arrange a meeting. He was not unpleasant but, nevertheless, made it very clear that in this way he was supposed to keep an eye on me. So, in this last year in Bulgaria, I was preoccupied with the question how I could leave the country, together with my family. I started preparing and waited for the big opportunity. Regardless, my life could have taken an unexpected turn. I applied for

8 Modern Hebrew

a position as an editor in the relatively new academic publishing house affiliated with the university. I had to take a written exam, together with another forty applicants. All of us knew in advance to whom the position would be given. However, three weeks after the person in question was hired, I got a job offer too. I had a permanent position for the first time in my life. I felt financially independent and secure. I got along with most of my colleagues, and my self-esteem was higher than ever. The editor-in-chief even mentioned the possibility to receive a leading position quite soon. I appeared to be at the beginning of a splendid career. To pursue a career was certainly not my highest goal. Nevertheless, I have to admit that being appreciated professionally aroused quite nice feelings in me. There were moments when I asked myself whether I would be ready to give up all this and to start all over again.

Everything was going very well until I had the naïve idea to organize a Bible reading circle. For about forty decades people in Bulgaria had been forbidden to read and to possess the Bible. The one single church bookstore in Sofia never had a copy and we could not borrow it in any library either. One could find only the old edition in Old Church Slavonic among friends or some of the very few copies of the edition published in London in Modern Bulgarian that were smuggled into the country illegally. A rumor that I was familiar with the Bible was spread around in relation to the translation of Thomas Mann's *Joseph and his Brothers* which I was editing. Some of my colleagues felt that it was unforgivable for intelligent people to be completely ignorant of the Bible and asked me if I could help. I was certainly willing to help. Soon, however, a question was raised: How come that I was interested in the Bible at all? That question came from all around: the man from the State Security, the party secretary in the publishing house, the bosses and their abettors. Someone had spilled the beans. To my surprise, this time there were no big accusations and no threats. Just the opposite! I was asked if I wanted to become a party member. The first time this question came up, I said only that I was not a well-organized person and that one could not rely on me in a kind of work like that. The second time, the female colleague who made me the offer was very clear:

"You should consider the fact that it is well known what kind of problems you had in the past," she said. "If you want to advance professionally and especially if you want to keep teaching at the university as well, then you better ask yourself whether it isn't about time to change something. Otherwise, you may not be allowed to educate young people."

I have my strong doubts that I would ever have been accepted as a member of the communist party, but this was indeed the usual method to make people feel indebted to the system. I was confronted with a clear dilemma: what was more important to me? Was I able to close my eyes and to forget everything that had ever meant a lot to me? Or would I rather give up a secure life and everything that I had built up so far?

I refused.

...

Meanwhile my colleagues in the publishing house had heard that I was offered membership in the party. From a professional perspective, my only disadvantage was the fact that I was not a party member. Had I become a member, I would have become quite able to compete. It was amusing to observe how some of my colleagues became afraid of my good qualities and started eagerly to make intrigues against me. The Human Resources department received anonymous letters, in which the authors called attention to my religious views and to my alleged involvement with sects antagonistic to the government. The game started all over again. I had no peace. I had to talk, to explain, to insist, and to justify myself again. It was clear to me that this would never end. I wanted out. I wanted to go away, as far as possible, just into the distance.

The problem, of course, was to get another travel permit. That was hopeless. When I traveled for the first time to the "West", I couldn't even imagine what it meant to report about the trip. Having that experience already, however, I was not ready to negotiate with the State Security or the secret service for the second time. Thus, I had to find a way to go around those institutions.

The solution came in the autumn of 1987. One of my colleagues had become a good friend. Once he shared with me that he had managed to help several friends of his to leave Bulgaria through a friend who worked in the passport department of the Ministry of Interior. He said that he himself would consider leaving Bulgaria. One day he came to me to ask for a favor. Many years before, the sister of the same friend of his from the passport department had been a law student at the university but never completed her degree. After such a long interruption she no longer had the right to take her state exams in order to graduate. The question was whether I could get the administration to make an exception, using the contacts I had as an assistant professor. This was my twelfth hour! It was the only way things could have worked out: I scratch your back, and you scratch my back. I agreed. I promised to do everything possible, on the condition that the brother of this woman would do me a favor too.

In Bulgaria passports did not belong to the citizens. If one wanted to go to the "West", they had to apply for a passport. There were two types of passports: official work passports and private passports. Three days after the end of each trip one had to return the passport to the authorities. Every time one wanted to travel, he/she had to apply for a travel permit anew. Only if the travel permit was approved could people get their passports again. I realized that there was no way the State Security would not be informed if I applied for a travel permit to the West. I also doubted it that I would ever get a passport for a second time. And even in the best scenario I would have received a passport again only if I had made certain promises. I did not want to have any obligations to the authorities. I had to find another option.

...

To travel to "the East" was generally much easier. Within the so-called Eastern Bloc we could travel with our ID card only. A loose sheet of paper with the exit and the entry visas for the countries we were supposed to visit was attached to it. Such trips were usually permitted by the Passport Department of the Interior Ministry and did not necessarily have to be approved by the State Security. I knew that in Belgrade there was a United Nations refugee camp. I also knew several people who had somehow managed to escape through the former Yugoslavia. However, in order to be permitted to travel through Yugoslavia, I also needed a *connection*. I explained to my colleague that I wanted to travel with my two children to Eastern Germany. Soon after, he told me that we could try to get a travel permit but under one condition, namely that I travel with one child only. The other one had to remain in the country as collateral.

I am not sure to what degree one can imagine the feelings of a mother confronted with such a dilemma. Perhaps most people do not have to make any dramatic choice between their children. Years later, many friends and relatives blamed me for being egoistic, even crazy, and for not having any feelings. Some despised or hated me for what I did. At some point, I myself wanted to give up the idea of escaping, for I loved my children more than anything.

When I became pregnant the first time, I knew that I was going to have a boy and that a good man was on his way to our world. I could feel the being that wanted to come, and I had a lot of respect for that being. I also had the feeling that I was observed, and I was very careful what I was doing, what I was saying and even thinking. I had a relatively difficult delivery. The doctors thought that we would not get away without a C-section. When I saw one of the resident doctors go to the other end of the room to bring the anesthesia mask, I despaired completely. Why, in God's name, did my boy have to come in such a way? Suddenly, I saw a young man standing next to me, to my left. He was sweet and very gentle. He put his hand on my feverish forehead and said: "It is over, Mom! Everything will be all right." Then I started screaming: "His hair, his hair . . . " The head of the baby was already out. I did not have a C-section. My first son came to the world. Somewhat bluish. A few more minutes passed before we heard his voice. He looked sad but beautiful. Today, when my son puts his hand on my forehead and says "Everything will be all right" I know that this is the same boy who stood next to me in the delivery room.

For lack of medical personnel, we, the young mothers, had to take care of our babies already in the first night after we gave birth. The babies were in little boxes behind a glass wall, next to the bed of each mother. My baby was crying very quietly, as if he was singing. I heard his voice and went to him. I was afraid to touch him, to wash him, to change his diapers and to wrap him. He was so tiny. I was just staring at him. When we look at the facial features of a baby it appears as if we could recognize in them the features of the adult person. Sages that have not yet broken their vows of silence. And he came out of me. I was his path. His help and support. I was responsible for him. Not he belonged to me but the other way round. I belonged to him. From now on and into eternity. As if I was allowed to host a special guest. It was fascinating. The gift of a friend, whom I had the honor to be taking care of and whom I was fortunate to be able to love. I loved him.

...

My husband and I were passionate mountaineers. Every year we spent many weeks in the mountains. We took our son to a mountain trek for the first time when he was five months old – in a backpack carrier on his father's back. After that, he almost always accompanied us in the mountains. He pronounced his first words in a hut we stopped at during a trek. Frequently, when we had difficult winter treks, the whole day we would hear only his voice, coming from his little backpack carrier seat, behind his father's shoulders: "Look, Mom, the sun is coming out again. Papa, be careful, the big water is coming. Can I sleep? Please, wake me up when we get down to the village. Papa, did you take the wrong trail again?"

One day, we were in a hut at about 2500 meters. It was in the spring. At this altitude, there was still snow cover everywhere. We were locked up in the mountain hut for about two days because outside there was a raging hurricane. On the third day the storm quieted down and we decided to move on. The snow cover was deep up to our knees. A thick fog was hanging over the jagged mountain crest. The trail to the next hut on the way down led over a very narrow spot on the slope. Dangerous cornices had built up on both sides of the precipice. I suffer fear of heights and have always been afraid of this spot. I wanted to go back. My husband, however, was not giving up. He continued walking and I followed. I was carrying the backpack and he our child. Just after we had passed this terrible spot the fog became so thick that the next marking pole was no longer to be seen. I stopped at one of the rare trees and my husband tried to find the way with his compass. Forty minutes later he gave up and said that we had to go back. Dusk was already falling. Frazzled snowflakes were falling silently from the sky. Everything was white. We could no longer distinguish between earth and sky. The fog entwined everything, and we stood there, exhausted and alone in the midst of this endless white wasteland. There was no trace of a mountain or a precipice. No trail. I sat down under the tree and did not want to get up again. I became silent and sleepy, and watched how the snow was covering my numb hands. I was ready to remain there. My husband was standing next to the tree and could barely notice what was happening to me for he himself had crossed the limits of his own endurance. Who knows what we were both waiting for! Then, suddenly, our son, who had been sleeping deeply for hours, woke up and said very quietly: "My hands and feet are freezing." I got up on my feet and started simply walking. I did not get dizzy and I was not afraid of the height. When I noticed that my husband could no longer stand on his feet, I took off my backpack, tied it to a tree, took my child on my back, and, without having exchanged a single word with my husband, started running downhill, hoping that I was running toward the hut. I ran and ran, fell down, got up quickly, and kept running again – until I saw the hut keeper coming toward us with a big sleigh. I woke up next morning. My feet were wrapped in goat skins. My husband and the hut keeper were sitting next to me, drinking tea. My son was crawling on the floor, his cheeks feverishly red, and he was alive and jolly.

Could I leave this child behind?

His little brother was then only seven. He was a child that brought us a lot of love. He was the spark of hope in an unhappy marriage – to all of us. Day after day, he somehow managed to keep reminding us that our life could be also beautiful. He brought us so much joy and changed our bad mood even when he was absolutely drained out himself. In the evening, he could never fall asleep before I read him a bedside story and gave him a kiss. At the time I was teaching at the university and sometimes I had lectures or seminars in the evening. If I was not at home before his bedtime, he had to have all his stuffed animals with him in his little bed and also something that belonged to me.

Who should I take and who should I leave? Or should I give up the future of all of us?

...

Usually, we misunderstand the idea of fate. We see it often as a sentence that hangs over us like Damocles' sword. To me, destiny was always just a road on which we walk, causing certain consequences by certain deeds. Our wishes and our intuition, however, are often intertwined. Sometimes we think that we have wished for something and that our wish is being fulfilled. But it may be just that we have walked in the right direction. One does not need to be a clairvoyant to feel intuitively what the consequences of an action might be. Our apprehensions could cause either a harmonious or a discordant state of mind. If we are aware of that state of mind, we believe we know what our future brings us. Sometimes we do things because we are in accord with others, and sometimes, it is simply *the voice of silence* that we trust.

I did not want my children to grow up in that country, in the same frustrating atmosphere as I had grown up in. I did not want them to live in fear, to be manipulated until they would be obsessed by the idea to grab a chance – any chance, regardless of what it was. What did responsibility mean in my case?

I had to move my older son to a different school when he was nine, because he did not want to let his teacher bully him. When he was little, I called him my Brown Bear. Once, by chance, I saw a very small brown teddy bear in a toy shop. I gave it to my son as a present and he wore it as a pendant on a thin leather band around his neck, usually hidden under his undershirt. It was his talisman. Once he was late for class. He had been playing soccer in the schoolyard and did not hear the bell. He was sweaty and had taken off his undershirt, intending to change in the classroom where he had left his shirt. However, when he got to the classroom, the teacher was already there. My son apologized and put on his shirt immediately. The teacher noticed his little teddy bear and got upset. My son, she said, was under Western influence, because he was wearing a necklace like the Heavy Metals – this was how people called any kind of punks at the time.

My son promised he would never wear his teddy bear over his clothes, so it was never going to be seen.

"Give it to me!"

"It is from my mother."

"Doesn't matter. It may be from your grandmother for what I care. Give it to me."

"But this is my talisman."

"All the more... give it to me or I'll kick you out."

"But why?"

"Because... Come on!"

The teacher ripped the leather band from my son's neck, took his teddy bear, and slapped him in the face.

On the next day I went to the school and asked for an explanation. The teacher said my son was unable to adjust to our society. I insisted that the whole story was too silly, and that she had no right to take away the boy's present from his mother in such a rude way. The teacher's answer to that was that it was impossible to bring up a child in the right way if the mother herself had such extreme ideas. She also said that she knew I myself was under certain particularly bad influences.

My son had just started second grade. At one of the first parents' conferences we were told that the school was going to introduce a new system designed to help children develop a sense of responsibility. The insane idea they were talking about was called "the vigilant eye." For that purpose, the school administration was supposed to select one child in each class but the rest of the children in that class were not supposed to know anything about it. The selected child was supposed to observe all other children in the class carefully – how they study, who cheats on tests, what games they play, what they talk about, what they say about their teachers and, more importantly, about their families, what upsets them, and what they laugh about. Every day, after the end of classes, that kid was supposed to remain in the school, without being noticed by other children, and was to report to the teacher about everything. That task was described as a particular honor and the selected children were promised their deserved appreciation by the teachers. We were discussing children in the age between seven and twelve.

...

Day after day I was changing my mind about which one of my two children I should take. I swore to myself that if I did not manage to get the other one out of Bulgaria too, I would go back. One day, my older son and I took a walk. We were talking about important things. My son had already heard conversations between his father and me concerning problems in Bulgaria, the difficulties we had, and possible plans of escape. We had even talked to him about those things because we wanted him to understand our dream of freedom. During our walk I told him about everything that was happening at the moment. I talked for about an hour and he kept silent. Then he said: "He is so little! In the evening, if you are not at home, he cries quietly, so that only I can hear him. He knows nothing about freedom. You cannot leave him here alone. He wouldn't understand this." My older son was then ten.

We decided together that it was the Little One that I should take. The Bigger One I had to promise that I would do everything in my power so that soon we would all be together again. It is difficult for me to explain why I was convinced that he was old and mature enough to comprehend the issue. In any case, the boy participated in the whole plan that followed, and that with amazing tact and sensitivity. When the Little One and I walked out from our home for the last time, his brother knew that he was not supposed to tell anyone where we were going and what was happening. He knew that if he said anything, I could still be stopped at the railway station or at the border, and I would be sent to prison. And he said not one word. The State Security wanted to get information about me from his father in the first place. They believed that I was involved with some anti-communist organization in the West and that I might have smuggled important archive materials out of the country. Apparently, there were people who also tried to grill my son. The boy sometimes saw neighbors eavesdropping at the door of our apartment, hoping to figure out something relevant from the conversations between father and son. My son could talk openly neither to friends nor to his closest relatives. He was afraid to speak openly even to his father at home for he realized that the apartment could have been bugged. Whenever other people were talking about me or about his father's plans for the future, he managed to deflect any suspicion that the two of them wanted to escape as well and to join us. He pretended to be calm and confident so that others wouldn't think that his mother's and his brother's disappearance mattered much to him. At the same time, he must have always been terribly afraid that some wrong word might slip out of his mouth. He was very sad, I have been told, but he also believed in me unconditionally. Six years later, after we had already been back together for some years, he read a few passages of this story and then he cried bitterly. For the first time. His brother and I were sitting silently next to him and did not even try to calm him down. And then he let it all out: "I was looking at you through the window as you were going down the street toward the bus stop. Your figures became smaller and smaller, until they disappeared in the fog. I was alone at home. I thought I would never see you again."

...

Back then I believed that I was to fulfill a task in the name of my children, and I was convinced that God would not have given me the chance to flee the country if that would have been wrong. I did not allow any doubts into my mind. Nevertheless, subconsciously, I must have felt terribly guilty because after I had already escaped and I was living in Tel Aviv, I was constantly dreaming of my older son whom I left behind in Bulgaria. His huge eyes with their astonished and sad look were following me everywhere. I was seeing him at the window of my room, I was waking up hearing his voice, and often, it took me a few minutes to be able to tell reality and dream apart. My skin remembered his thick hair, my fingers felt his little hand that I always held in mine when we took a walk, and I could sculpt his little body out of the air.

One evening, I was sitting on the terrace in our asylum in Tel Aviv. The jasmine trees were already in blossom and the night was thick, full of the scent of jasmine. The city was silent and dark. The Little One had fallen asleep. I was alone on the terrace and was aware only of the salty humidity and the scent of the trees. Nature is gentle in its own way. When the sun is shining in the morning or when we draw fresh water from a well, we may feel blessed in a way. My intoxicating night back then gave me a blessing. It sat down next to me and laid its calm around my shoulders. I rested my head on its body, closed my eyes, and fell into a slumber. And then I saw the huge eyes of my older son looking at me. It was so beautiful! I was glad and everything was so harmonious. I felt his hands on my arm. I was so lucky to be able to feel him so close to me. If I could only diminish the distance! How was it that he was with me and not with me? What was there in between? Land, or just my mind? Where was I really – with him or on the terrace?

A few years earlier I had been once again in the mountains with my children and some friends. It was in the spring. We wanted to climb a summit. At that altitude the snow cover was everywhere at least two, three meters or about seven to ten feet. Since the crust might have started to melt around noon, we got up at five in the morning and wanted to reach our goal by midday. The snow, however, was very soft and we could barely walk. The entire route was in the open, directly exposed to the sun. There was no forest, not a single tree. We needed about seven hours to reach the summit. All the time we were able to see the trail we had broken and left behind. In that area the mountains had very soft shapes. No cliffs, no abysses. No hills that were too high. Just snow dunes. If one does not see any colors and everything around glitters in an even white, the landscape seems to be pretty monotonous. One loses the sense for perspective and, thus, for distance too. Every time we looked back that day, it was as if we had not moved at all. When, after seven hours of walking, we finally stood at the summit, I had a unique experience. I was able to see the precise spot where we had started early in the morning. This spot was just next to us, in the place where we were standing now too. Nevertheless, it was also seven hours away from us. We were completely exhausted from the long trekking through the snow. For our bodies, the starting point was very far away. At the same time we could see it clearly – close enough to touch. This was absolute relativity of time and space. This was incomprehensible for the mind but very clear to the senses.

The distance that separated me from my son disappeared. I was able to overcome it in my thoughts. At that time I learned that our mind has more power than all the governments in the world. No law or anything else in the world could have separated me from my son, for he was with me, and by that I mean much more than my memory of or my love for him.

Charter 77

When I got off the train in Belgrade with the Little One on that first morning after my escape, the heavy, gloomy autumn was hanging over the train station. I was standing in a perfectly normal train station, with tracks and platforms, with halls and buildings, and nothing was normal anymore. On the inside, I was torn to pieces and I did not know what to do. I felt no excitement and I could make no plans. All my dreams and ideals seemed to have crumbled like a sandcastle in the rising tide and I did not have the vaguest idea of the future. I was standing in the midst of a murky uncertainty and I was full of fear. I could only squeeze my son's hand as I stared, numb, into the distance.

I had to pull myself together when my son said that he was hungry. At this critical moment of my life I was able to think only in very basic terms. I wanted to open the door to the kitchen and to put the milk pot on the stove. I wanted to do this as calmly as I had been doing it for years, every single morning. However, there was no milk pot at all and, slowly, I began to realize what was happening.

What I felt had nothing to do with my thinking or with the fact that psychologically I was prepared for the escape. I had feelings that seem to surface when one is in shock, and that are related to our deepest and most basic reflex-like habits. At that moment, standing at the train station, I discovered a technique that helped me over and over again, throughout this entire difficult period of time. Every time when a situation became extremely complicated, I held on to the most banal, most concrete, and most practical things such as cleaning, making salad, or washing dishes very thoroughly. Doing things like that helped me gain back the sense of normality and stop feeling the painful pressure of the extreme. By dealing consciously with the specifics of a particular action, which normally I would perform automatically, I was becoming more able to think about the details of any given problem and to separate the wheat from the chaff.

I looked around to see if there was some foreign exchange window at the train station. There was one, but I had not considered the fact that my Bulgarian money would be totally useless. In the only existing bank in Bulgaria, the National Bank, I was allowed to exchange a very limited amount of money, and only for GDR currency, since this was where I was supposed to travel to. My request to receive part of the money in Yugoslav currency was rejected with the explanation that I was only going to be passing through Yugoslavia and, thus, I should not need any local money. This was one of the small tricks used to prevent people from any potential attempt to escape through Yugoslavia. On that first morning at the train station in Belgrade I thought I was going to faint. I was standing there, with my little child, and could not get a penny for my Bulgarian money to buy breakfast, not to speak of doing anything else. I tried to exchange my GDR money, but the result was the same. It was over with this plan. I had no chance. Just stay calm, I said to myself and remained standing there to think. Then suddenly a voice asked me if I was looking for something. In front of me there was a short man. Bald, with small fingers. At 8 o'clock in the morning. I said I was looking for a bank where I could exchange Bulgarian or East German money. The man laughed and told me that there was no bank where I could do anything with my money, but that he might be able to find another way. He wanted to invite us first to breakfast in some café, though. We went to the café. It was warm and cozy. The man ordered a big hearty breakfast for us, sat down quietly while we were eating, and slowly smoked his cigarette. When we were ready, he explained that there were truck drivers who drove frequently through the border to Bulgaria and who sometimes might exchange Bulgarian money. However, early in the morning, the truck drivers would hang out in a very dodgy area where he could not go with me and the child. He suggested that I should give him my money and wait for him in the café. My money may well not have had any value in Yugoslavia, but it was all the money I had. Nevertheless, I did not hesitate even for a second. I gave the man the money and he left. About forty minutes later he came back and brought me Yugoslav dinars. He accompanied us to the city center, where I wanted to go, said goodbye, and disappeared in a bus.

First, I wanted to call a friend who was living in the West and who could advise me what was possible to do in Belgrade in order to escape. I expected him to give me addresses, contacts – a real escape plan. I could not dare to call him from Bulgaria.

Years ago, when the population of Bulgaria was seven million people, a great satire writer, Radoy Ralin, wrote in an epigram that Bulgaria had seven million telephones and seven million microphones. I did not know if every single telephone was tapped but I knew for sure that each international phone call was intercepted. It was unthinkable to discuss an escape plan over the phone.

I made the phone call. My friend could not be reached. He was on vacation.

Bad luck!

I had to find a solution.

I called an old acquaintance whom I had visited thirteen years before in Novi Sad. He was very surprised, but he immediately invited us to his place. He lived just outside the city. We took the train to him. It took me a lot of time to find his place because I could not remember anything. Meanwhile it started to rain. It was already late afternoon. We arrived wet and tired and it was warm in his home. Our host let my boy watch TV in the living room. He and I sat down in his small sweet kitchen. We chatted for a while about common friends in Sofia, about who was still married and who was divorced, about who was still alive and who died. Then the question came up, what I was actually doing there. I had to tell him what I was planning. While I was still talking, I noticed concern in his eyes. He pulled a long face and wanted to express his opinion. I wanted to preempt his statement and said that I needed his help only for a few days – until I could figure out what the possibilities were.

No! It was impossible. He was a party member and a professor at the university. If by chance any of his neighbors came to suspect something, they would report him to the police immediately.

What he was saying made sense. By law, he would have been obliged to register a foreign guest with the police. Otherwise, he really could have been in trouble. The man was simply afraid, and I did not want to cause problems for him.

I remembered another friend from Bulgaria who was living at the moment in Sweden. I knew that a few years ago he had escaped from Bulgaria through Yugoslavia. He was not on vacation. I explained the situation briefly. He exclaimed: “Oh, dear God!” and moved on to practicalities. He wanted me to hang up. Ten minutes later he called back and said that a good friend of his from Belgrade was willing to help. He could pick us up on the next morning. My host said no. Early on the next morning his cleaning lady was supposed to come, and she must not find us in his place. We had to leave. Late that evening, around nine, we took the train back to Belgrade to go to the friend of my friend from Sweden. It would have been impossible for us to find an address in an unknown neighborhood. I stopped a taxi and had to pay the driver with the rest of the exchanged money I had.

...

We walked in around eleven.

This was a nice family: a high school teacher with two children. They were all still awake and were waiting for us. They had prepared a nice supper and, after the children had long fallen asleep, we kept chatting until late. The husband was well informed in politics and had a pretty good idea about the situation in Bulgaria. We liked each other and I felt that these people had real understanding for what we were going through. The man was ready to bring us to the UN refugee camp on the following day and said that we were always welcome visiting them, but only in the evening, and we had to be very careful that the neighbors did not see us. Often, when we went to see these people, we had to walk around the block several times, until the air was clear and we were not afraid to enter their house. We found a nice and friendly atmosphere in this home. The young family helped us with advice and also with food in the beginning, since we were getting only breakfast in the UN refugee camp. Most importantly, my son could play with their children, and we had someone to talk to.

Outside, on the streets, I was afraid to talk to my son. I was concerned that someone might realize we were speaking Bulgarian, and who knows what could have happened then. I heard stories about people who were kidnapped in Belgrade by the Bulgarian secret service and brought back to Bulgaria through the border very quickly. At the end of the day, it was a matter of only a few kilometers. This fear, typical for people from communist countries, predominated everywhere in Belgrade. The air had literally the stench of fear. From the very first moment when I decided to escape, I felt as if I was a conspirator. I was plotting when I was making a phone call abroad, I was plotting when I had to apply for an exit visa, and I was plotting when I was buying our train tickets. Going through customs was another hotbed of plotting and, under the circumstances, I was gradually turning into a big plotter who, in reality, wanted simply to move from point A to point B. However, with crossing the Bulgarian border, the story was far from over.

I believe that this conspiratorial spirit has a damaging effect on the psyche of a person that can be overcome, if at all, only by a very, very strong will. I became aware of this for the first time about a year later.

I was already living in Germany. I was travelling, together with a female friend, on the overnight train from Munich to Rome to help with the illegal escape of my husband and my older son. The most important part of my role in this operation was to prove to the Italian and to the German border authorities that I was a German citizen, and that, in our case, this was a question of family reunion. Thus, it was extremely important to have all my documents with me. Already at the time when my German passport was issued, I thought that I could not possess anything more precious than this document. It represented my life, my freedom, my goal, and my dream. Simply everything. For many months after I received my passport I had a frequently recurring nightmare when I was sleeping: I was back in Bulgaria and they had taken away my German passport; I could not prove that I was a German citizen and I was not allowed to leave the country – as before. I always woke up sweating and breathless, and started looking for my passport. Only when I had it in my hands again could I calm down and fall asleep again. That night, in the train to Rome, when I had to leave Germany for the first time and to travel abroad, I had my passport in my underwear. My friend wanted to have both passports ready for border control and she had to see where I had hidden mine. She was appalled. She told me directly, that I should leave my communist traumas behind. I was terribly offended and blamed her for not having any understanding for people like me. But she was right. This was sick.

When I finally got to the UN refugee center in Belgrade, they sent me to their camp, and they gave me an interview appointment. In two weeks.

The camp was a bit isolated, in a little forest. It consisted of wooden bungalows and a small administrative building with a dining hall. They took all our papers and gave us a double bungalow. It was mid-October. Cold and wet. There was no heating in the rooms. The Little One was exhausted. I wanted him to go to bed but he couldn't fall asleep and begged me to stay with him. I laid down next to him. It was around four o'clock in the afternoon on the third day after we left Bulgaria. We slept until eleven the following morning.

...

Narrow unpaved walkways led through the woods to the bungalows. One could barely see the camp from the street. There was no sound coming from that direction either. No voices, no music. The curtains on most windows were closed and no door was ever left open. Every now and then human silhouettes appeared on the walkways. If people wanted to greet one another at all, they only nodded their heads briefly and moved on. This was not a refugee camp of the sort we have in the West. People didn't want to exchange information and had no desire to get to know each other. In the morning, at breakfast, one could only hear the clear clink of teaspoons touching china cups. Tired shadows with no voices and no names dragged themselves slowly through the compound. As in a ghost town. People were afraid. I think that the specific character of the refugee camp in Yugoslavia was determined by the intermediate position of that country. Earlier, when refugee camps existed only in the West, to reach the West meant to have reached freedom. No matter with how many difficulties one was confronted, one probably felt safe anyway. In the '80s, Yugoslavia was an "*as-well-as*," or rather a "*neither-nor*" country. On the one hand the UN refugee camp did exist there, but on the other hand, local people were strictly forbidden to talk and to give any information about it. Refugees would receive a document that guaranteed the protection of the UN. However, it was known that there were Serbs who would sometimes kidnap refugees and return them to the neighboring socialist countries for money. Rumor had it that even the Yugoslav police and border patrol carried out orders given by the communist governments of other countries from the Eastern Bloc. In this atmosphere of secrecy and conspiracy, fear got the better of me too and I panicked, thinking that someone might recognize us and bring us back to Bulgaria.

In the midst of this amorphous mass of refugees in the camp, there was only one single person who paid some attention to us and who kindly befriended my son. It was a Romanian boy of fifteen. His parents had already been in the States for a year. When his family tried to cross the border between Romania and Hungary, he stayed behind because he did not want to abandon his little brother, who had been caught by the border guards. The parents must have realized too late what was happening, and they simply kept going. The two brothers were sent to prison in Romania but were soon released because they were minors. Two more times they tried to cross the border and two more times they were locked up in prison. Until they finally succeeded. When I met him, they had already been in Yugoslavia for nine months and they were waiting for their entry visa to the U.S., from where the parents were sending them, on a regular basis, pictures of the pretty little house in which they lived.

Other than that, everybody was silent around the camp, the refugees as well as the Serbs working there.

...

I remember sitting at the dinner table of our Belgrade friends one night. We had just started to eat when the doorbell rang. Our friends panicked. We had to get off the table right away. Our plates and utensils were immediately put away and we were locked in a room so that no one could discover us. The people who came were neighbors and friends of the family. As people may visit each other unannounced on the Balkans, these neighbors remained there for about three hours. The living room was at the other end of the hallway. We could hear them talk even through the two doors that separated us. It was cold in our room. We were not supposed to turn on the lights and we could not go to the bathroom. During those three hours I had to play Scheherazade to distract my son from thinking about his needs. Until he fell asleep, exhausted from the sheer pain in his bladder.

We were not supposed to be even like shadows. We had no shapes and no voices. And we kept quiet. Every day, we looked for a quiet place where we could talk to each other. The rest of the time we were numb.

For various reasons, my son had to keep silent for a very long time. In Yugoslavia, so that people did not hear him speak Bulgarian. Later, in Italy, so that no one would come up with the idea to ask us for our papers, for we had none; In Israel, because initially he knew no language in which he could communicate with others; and then when we finally arrived in Germany and he already spoke some German, he was not supposed to open his mouth when we were looking to rent an apartment, so that no one could figure out from his accent that we were foreigners. It is not difficult to imagine what it meant for an eight-year-old intelligent and lively child to keep his mouth shut so often and for such long periods of time. Eventually, he started producing some strange sounds and several years had to pass before this kind of a nervous tic disappeared.

While we were in Yugoslavia, I heard the Little One laugh loud and jolly only one single time. It was on his birthday. How were we supposed to celebrate it?

Yugoslav goods counted as Western in Bulgaria. They did not have high quality, but they were colorful and shiny. Children looked with big bewildered eyes when someone had a chewing gum or something similar from Yugoslavia. With the few pennies I found in the pocket of my jacket I bought my son a small pack of chewing gums. I lit a match, holding it over the packet, and sang "Happy Birthday" for him. He laughed. He was happy. He understood what that meant. And I knew that with this boy I would never be alone.

...

I was quite confused when I realized how things worked in Yugoslavia and that, depending on the circumstances, we might have had to wait for about a year before we were permitted to emigrate to any state in the West. I had never considered the possibility of staying there that long – with no school for the Little One, with no money, and so close to Bulgaria. I wanted to leave as soon as possible, and I started what I called "my huge embassy project." I went first to the German embassy. I was welcomed in a very kind manner, but I was told that Germany is not an immigration country. Only people of German origin were accepted into the country. Since I had no documents that could prove my German origin, they said they could not help me. No one explained to me what exactly I could have done to prove that I came from a German family. I was simply politely sent away.

I remember that in the beginning of the '90s, about six years after I had escaped, the refugees from the former Eastern Bloc were so well informed that they were able to book their trip up to the door of the asylum shelter from their homes, including the smuggler. When I escaped, I did not know anything about immigration and non-immigration countries, or about the differences between expats, immigrants, and expellees. I was quite surprised that a refugee may not enter certain countries in the free world. It was a real shock. What was I to do?

At that time my father had long been dead. I loved him very much and I trusted his opinion so completely that every time when I had to make a difficult decision I tried to think what he would have advised me to do. I remembered then when I travelled for the first time to Eastern Germany, age eighteen, my father gave me a tip. He said: "If you are abroad and you do not know how to deal with something, go to the local Jewish community center and ask for advice." I searched the phone book, talked to people on the streets, asked in hotels and at the train station. No one in Belgrade knew anything about a Jewish community center or about a Synagogue. It seemed impossible that there was no Jewish organization there but obviously it was so secretive that perhaps only the Yugoslav Secret Service would know where it was. I do not remember any longer how I came up with the idea to ask in the American Embassy. The receptionist at the door realized immediately what this was about. She looked at some list, gave me the address and the phone number, and explained to me how to get there.

Considering the cold atmosphere of mistrust typical for the Jewish community in Sofia, I had my doubts about the one in Belgrade. The center was located on the second floor of an old building, a little bit remote but in a nice neighborhood. There were only a few people there. We were invited to see the chairperson, a friendly woman, probably around fifty. She was observing me very carefully but was quite sweet to my son. I told her briefly our story. Her face looked more and more concerned with each word I said. She lit one cigarette after the other and did not interrupt me one single time. When I finished, she buried her face in her hands and kept silent for a while.

We had to wait for the interview in the UN. However, the Jewish community supported us financially throughout the entire time we spent in Belgrade. Already the first time we showed up there they gave us money for food. They kept asking us again and again if we had enough to eat and if we needed anything else. I felt better and I felt safer. What was even more important was that my son had the feeling we were no longer completely lost in that city. Ever since I met these people I have been thinking about them, every day, and I have been grateful that they existed.

Two weeks later I had my interview. I had never heard anything about such hearings before. I said everything I had to say briefly and simply. The nice gray-haired Swedish lady who was interviewing me kept nodding her head in a sign of understanding and before I left said: "I hope very much that we can help you." She asked me also where I wanted to go. Being completely ignorant I specified precisely the two countries I should never have mentioned – Germany and Israel. There were two cultures in the world that were close to me – the German and the Jewish. German literature and the history of the Jewish people had shaped my entire consciousness. I had close friends and relatives in Germany and in Israel. And I had a child with me whose lost home I wanted to replace as soon as possible. It could have never crossed my mind to emigrate to Sweden or Australia, and America sounded terribly far from my older son. Germany, however, was not an immigration country, and the United Nations were very sensitive with regard to Israel. There were two big Jewish organizations in the world – the Jewish Agency, responsible for bringing Jews to Israel, and HIAS, in charge of Jews going to the United States. The United Nations did not want to have any dealings with the work of either one.

I received an answer around four in the afternoon. Rejection. The Swedish lady explained to me that her boss found my application for asylum unfounded. Among all other points I had made, I had also mentioned that because of my problems with the state security it had been very difficult for me to find a permanent job. This point of my statement was taken out of its context and it was presented in a very twisted way as if I was unemployed. Thus, my reasons to apply for asylum were treated not as political but as economic and this turned out to be fatal. In fact, when I decided to escape, I had a permanent position as an editor in one of the most prominent academic publishing houses. In addition, I was a part time German language instructor at the University, and I was also a well-known translator. Nevertheless, the requirements of the letter of the law had to be satisfied. They had to find an explanation for the rejection, even if it did not correspond to the facts.

I stood there speechless.

The lady said she was terribly sorry that she could not help me and I believed her. I could see that in her eyes. She realized that I was uninformed and desperate. When I was saying goodbye, she hinted very carefully that, depending on the circumstances, I could cross the Yugoslav border illegally, yet she also stressed that she had no right to advise me to do that. Luckily, she did it anyway.

. . .

When I returned with my Little One to the camp around six o' clock in the evening, we found out what had happened there meanwhile. Our room was emptied. There were no sheets on the bed any longer. My stuff was thrown into a small pile outside, in front of the door. Towels, underwear, clothes. A hefty guy who was on duty as a watchman was leaning at the wall of the administrative building. He grinned at me and announced that we could no longer sleep there. Since we had not received an asylum status, the United Nations had not covered the cost for room and board. I had to pay for the two weeks myself in order to get my papers back. If I remember correctly, this was about three hundred and twenty US dollars. I had left Bulgaria with thirty lev and a hundred and twenty GDR marks. To me my debt to the camp sounded like an astronomical amount of money and I had no idea what to do.

It was already evening, and I was kicked out on the street with my child. Keep calm, I thought, and tried to pull myself together. I packed the little luggage we had and called our friends in Belgrade.

We spent the night with them. On the following day I received the necessary amount of money from the Jewish community center and I was able to release our petty papers.

Unfortunately, I cannot report how we came across the border. We were helped by people who risked their freedom and a lot more than that. People like us. I can only say that emotionally it was horrible for me. Later, friends have told me that I must have been very strong and very brave back then. This is not true. I cannot describe in words the fear I experienced. I was a bundle of feelings and of faith. It was as if we consciously jumped into an abyss and expected nevertheless to wake up in one piece in another world.

And we did wake up.

...

A year later, I visited a friend in Aachen and we drove quickly to the Netherlands to buy coffee there. The coffee from Holland, she said, tasted better and had a finer scent. It was raining. At the border, there was a small watchman's cabin which was empty and locked. It took us ten minutes to buy the coffee in a small shop on the highway and to drive back to Germany. I sat down on the ground at this border between Germany and the Netherlands, in the rain, and I cried. I cried with bitter tears. For myself, for all the children, brothers, parents, and dreamers on whom the Iron Curtain had imposed that incomprehensible insanity. The Iron Curtain was not only at the borders. It was ingrained deep down in all of us and it had shaped the lives of many people. It had hurt and damaged us, and it had turned the personalities of those who tried to oppose it into a crazy gridlock web, from which only a few were later able to stitch together something like a dignified human consciousness.

Roma Bene

The very first thing I experienced in the West consciously was an Italian bath. I was completely drained out by the events of the last two weeks. After two terrible days when we had to hide in all sorts of holes so that no one could discover us, I was lying in a bathtub in beige. The water smelled like fresh forest moss and I was enjoying the hot steam that penetrated my skin and made my body feel soft. It was quiet and I felt safe. It was over with a whole world which I had left behind. My son was watching cartoons on the television in the living room. As if life has just begun anew. From the very beginning.

We came to Rome by night-train. The Little One slept all the way through but I could not even close my eyes because I was afraid someone might ask me for my papers.

I had often dreamed of Rome. I was in love with antiquity and knew quite well where different sights were. I had wanted so much to see this city. However, when I was finally right there and could have admired it, I felt mentally so empty that each beautiful view could only make me sad. I felt guilty that I was able to see all this without my older son. It was as if I had deprived him of something. The more wonderful my impressions were, the emptier I felt. Why was my boy denied all this? Why couldn't I show him everything? Why were there two worlds anyway?

We stood on St. Peter's Square, in front of the Vatican, absolutely quietly, charmed by the fascinating view. I felt for the first time that the endless expanse which all my life I had carried hidden inside myself could assume tangible forms not only in the mountains but also down here, in the world of stone and walls.

What kind of people are the ones that have grown up in buildings like that?

Like organ music, the Roman architecture expanded my inner space into the incomprehensible. What I had known from art albums was fiction. One cannot capture on paper the memory of a city that radiates from every corner.

This was the faraway world that I had dreamed of – always having had the desire to see and feel something completely different. I did not know what it must have been. I knew only that it would make me expand and that I would feel well, as when I watched the sea from the shore. I knew that I would take small steps slowly, to feel the cool water touch my feet; that I would feel the skin of the water with my entire body and I would want to immerse myself in its depth. The waves would have taken me along and they would have surely carried me, without me having any fear. I never knew where this thing might be, but I knew it had to be in the far away world, in the beyond. Now, I was standing in the middle of it. The beyond was in front of my eyes.

. . .

The Little One was exhausted and I was not sure how much longer he could endure the situation. I needed help. I had been told that in most big cities in the West there is a representation of the Jewish Agency. I found it.

The building was impressive. It was barred, locked, secured, and protected. The conversation I had in the Jewish Agency was my first contact with a Western institution, if I do not count the United Nations in Belgrade. In Bulgaria, every time I had to go to some government office, I felt as if I was accused of a crime and I had to appear in court. I believe that most people there felt the same way. We all had to justify ourselves for having had to appear in the office in the first place. After that, we had to be prepared to be harassed in different ways. Public office offered a unique opportunity for acting out social inferiority complexes through the use of power. We depended on every unimportant official, and the officials knew how to make use of this. Regardless whether one had to ask for some out-of-stock goods in a shop or wanted to buy tickets for a guest performance, or even worse, if one had to ask for some documents to be issued, one always felt guilty and dependent. We were all harassed and sent away, until we were willing to beg, to suck up to and to bribe the respective officials.

As we entered through the locked iron gate of the building of the Jewish Agency I felt quite uncomfortable. While I was explaining to the woman-secretary what this was about, another woman brought my son sweets, juice, and a children's magazine. We were invited immediately to the director's office. He listened to me carefully, asked brief questions, looked very serious but smiled too, in a very friendly way. His questions were structured in such a different way. They did not aim at exposing me and they did not represent any traps, as I would have expected it in Bulgaria. Over the course of this conversation I gradually lost my fear of officials and was surprised to realize that people actually wanted to help me. The director not only showed compassion but he was also extremely respectful and treated me as an equal. At this particular moment my destiny and the destiny of my son were literally in his hands, but he conversed with me in a way that did not make me feel dependent. A new feeling rose in me, a feeling of human dignity. I realized that the way I was treated had an immediate effect on the way I behaved.

My conversation with the director of the Jewish Agency in Rome made me aware of another aspect of the mental crippling occurring in communist societies. In daily life people were constantly treated as if they were inferior. As a consequence, they felt psychologically dependent and, not having any self-esteem and being full of fear, they had to beg for everything. Gradually, a society was established which consisted mostly of social beggars. At the same time, there existed more or less important privileged positions that offered oppressed people the possibility to oppress others. From a psychological viewpoint the worst was not the high-level oppression exercised by the communist party but the fact that people could oppress each other on all sorts of marginal levels in their daily life. This was a vicious circle where it was very difficult to cultivate unharmed, self-confident personalities with a healthy spirit. In communist Bulgaria the total exhaustion leading to submissiveness was used as means of exercising power in all possible areas of social life, including in the military.

A good friend of my first husband told the story of the invasion of Czechoslovakia in 1968 in which Bulgarian troops joined the Soviets. The invasion happened shortly before our friend was supposed to be discharged from his mandatory military service. One night there was alarm in his regiment. The soldiers were told this was an exercise. For a few days they had to move every night, without knowing where to. Then, for a period of time of three whole days they stayed in a marshland where they had to sleep literally in the mud. When they were told that they were at the border with Czechoslovakia and that, in the name of the republic, they had to defend the holy idea of communism against a fascist upheaval, most of the soldiers were in such a terrible condition that they were ready to do anything, just so that they could get away from this goddamned spot. In addition, the participants in this shameful deployment of the lust for power were promised that upon return they would be admitted as students in any discipline and at any university, without the usual entry exam.

After the director of the Jewish Agency asked me what kind of help I would expect from them and pointed out various possibilities, I requested that they put me in touch with the Israeli embassy.

Our arrival at the embassy caused total panic. A woman with a child, without a passport, without a past, and she was coming from a clearly hostile country. People started making phone calls, sending faxes, writing notes. A while later we had our entry permission for Israel in our hands. However, we were warned that we would have overcome all the obstacles only after we had passed the border control at the airport. A room in one of the best hotels in Rome and two tickets for the first airplane to Tel Aviv on the next morning were booked for us.

That evening we went for a walk. In the first place I wanted to call my friend in Jerusalem and let him know that the Little One and I would soon arrive in Israel. This time I did reach him. He was so glad to hear that and asked me if I was happy too. I was painfully missing my older son; I felt responsible for the destiny of the Little One; I was afraid of what awaited us; and I was completely exhausted. I could not describe myself as being happy.

Early next morning a young woman and a young man from the agency took us to the airport. The atmosphere there was terrifying. All around, there were policemen in black. They were carrying machine guns and were ready to shoot. I have been at the airport in Rome many times later and I do believe that there must have been a very special reason for this at the time because I did not have the same impression ever again. Back then, one could have thought that a terrible shooting spree would occur at any moment. I was holding my boy tightly by the hand and we went to the border control. We had no passports, no visas for Italy – just the laissez passer for Israel. We were coming simply from nowhere. The young man behind the glass window looked at our strange papers and asked how we had entered his country. I was so scared that I could not produce a sound. The man thought

I could not understand him. He tried repeating "documenti, documenti." Then it clicked. This was it! I should pretend that I did not understand him. I stared at him stupidly and pointed at the documents in his hand. He did not give up and tried this time French and English, asking repeatedly if I had an entry visa for Italy. I was dumbfounded and pale like a marble statue, and I was praying that, somehow, we would get through. The man got upset. He pointed to the spot in the Israeli laissez passer where it said that I was born in Bulgaria and he started yelling: "Bulgaria, Roma", showing with his fingers that we must have walked somehow from Bulgaria to Italy. I nodded with my head one more time in a most stupid way and looked him directly in the eyes. Surprisingly, he made a gesture with his hand – something that must have meant "go to hell!" and he pushed our papers back to us. I was not sure whether he wanted to let us through or not. When I opened the door to the transit area I felt as if I was somewhere between existence and non-existence, and everything seemed to be unreal.

"What's the matter, Mami?" said the Little One and, all of a sudden, I was standing again with both feet on the ground.

Everything related to an El-Al flight is always thoroughly checked. Just, that I did not know all this back then. We were all already sitting in the plane and the engines were running. Suddenly, my name was called through the loudspeaker and I was asked to come out.

"It is over," I thought, and my knees started trembling. When I was coming down the steps, I saw our rucksacks lying on the ground outside. Didn't they want to let us fly? The security people asked me only if I had packed everything by myself and if I would double check my luggage one more time. Then they apologized and I went back into the plane.

Full of hope we said goodbye to Rome.

Ba Aretz[9]

I do not think that anywhere else in the world immigrants are welcomed the way they are welcomed in Israel.

My friend from Jerusalem came to Tel Aviv to be there when we arrived at the airport Ben Gurion. Immediately after we arrived we were led into a big room. On a table, I saw an old Russian copper samovar, non-alcoholic beverages, and sweets. An official from the Sochnut, the Jewish Agency in Israel, greeted us and congratulated us with having come home. For people like my son and myself, who had lost everything, this sounded fascinating.

Outside, however, life was waiting for us.

On both sides of the motorway going from the airport to Tel Aviv there were date palms. It was the first time the Little One saw palm trees. For a long time after that he kept drawing palm trees. One day a year later, shortly before we left Israel, he ran to each palm we saw, hugged it, and said goodbye.

I had many relatives and friends in Israel but usually each newcomer to the country, or each *ole hadash,* had to stand on his/her own feet and to start from the very beginning. It was possible to receive shelter in an asylum home and normally immigrants did take that opportunity.

In fact, one cannot compare the asylum homes for immigrants in Israel, the *beth olim*, to the refugee camps of the United Nations or the shelters for asylum seekers in Europe. The *beth olim*, the homes for immigrants in Israel, were situated everywhere in big, nice, and clean buildings in the most modern parts of the respective cities. The apartments were designed either for one or two people or for a whole family. Each apartment had a small kitchenette with refrigerator and a cooker, and a small bathroom with a toilet and a shower cabin. In addition, there were always a communal room and an events hall on the first floor. In the first two months newcomers had to deal with all sorts of arrangements. However, no one had to waste time running from office to office and waiting forever in front of different doors. Institutions such as social services, employment agencies, and health insurance, were represented in the building. Some of them had an office

9 The land of Israel.

in the home and others would have office hours there once or twice a week. The language courses of Modern Hebrew or Ivrit, the *Ulpanim*, were organized on location too. In addition to taking five hours language classes a day, one could also get help from a professional tutor. Usually, the *beth olims* were located in the middle of a development complex where there were also a bank, at least two supermarkets, a polyclinic, and a school. Children, as well as elderly people, and generally everyone who needed more time to settle in a new environment, had the opportunity to organize their new lives very easily, without feeling lost. Regardless of the political reasons for the state of Israel to invest so much money in immigrants, this country has created an exemplary model for their integration.

There is a proverbial phrase that Israelis often tell the *olim*, most of whom really hate it. If one grasps its deep meaning, however, one could move mountains by using this concept. *Savlanut* – Patience. To be patient without being passive. Whatever one wanted to achieve, one had to work towards that goal every single minute, investing all the energy one had, nevertheless being aware of the fact that everything needs time. Big things come to us only if we slowly move towards them.

Our apartment was on the second floor of the *beth olim* and had a pretty large terrace as well. Often, before the rain season started, my son and I sat there on the warm autumn evenings, and we dreamed of the future. Differently from the usually dry landscape of the country, Tel Aviv was a green city, full of trees and flowers. Under our terrace there was a small park with a playground and many jasmine trees. We became fully aware of them only in the following spring when they began to spread their intoxicating fragrance. Opposite the park there was only a small school building, so that our view was not obscured. The deep blue color of the sky over Tel Aviv appeared often to be so alive that it was possible to think one could relate to it as to a living being.

About a month after we arrived in Israel the first *Intifada* began. It is extremely difficult to speak of fear and danger when you live in that country. In Israel children grow up with fear and danger. Thus, they are also treated like royalties. There are laws that protect children from everything and from everybody, including from their own parents. No one spelled this out, but everyone was aware of the fact that the children of today may not live longer than seventeen years – that is, until they are drafted.

Those days I knew very little about international politics. What I was able to feel and to grasp were the human circumstances. And what I felt was that this country had been living with the war uninterruptedly, for many, many years. Danger is part of every-day life in Israel. However, it appeared that one could not live constantly in fear. Consciously or subconsciously people seemed to develop some kind of a survival instinct. They were laughing and having fun, and they were happy, despite the fact that they had just heard of the last bomb explosion. To me, the entire attitude toward fear and suffering people in Israel had was something completely new. I grew up in an authoritarian dictatorship where crime was not so high, and the streets were famously safe. I did not even know what homeless people or prostitutes were. Not because there weren't any there but because the streets in the big cities were cleared of them and because they were never discussed in the media. I was confused in Israel. I did not know how to deal with fear.

One day my son got sick in Tel Aviv. He had high fever and I did not let him go to school. He was going to the school just across from us. Around noon I heard loud voices under the terrace. A voice over a loudspeaker said that the school compound had to be cleared immediately. I looked from the terrace and saw many police officers with gas masks and some weapons. They detonated a bomb in the school. No one was hurt. But the Little One might have been there. And the bomb might have exploded. In the following two months I was afraid to take a walk. I did not want to take the bus and I barely agreed to send my son to school again. When we went grocery shopping, I held him tightly by the hand. I was afraid of every single moment when I had to be separated from him.

Until Purim came.

Everybody wanted to celebrate the holiday and people were looking for costumes. There were supposed to be bonfires on the streets and children wanted to sing and dance. I had to let go of my son. I could not spoil his holiday. He left home with his friends, went who knows where, and came back about seven hours later. After that, we started living like everybody else. We travelled through the country and we went to the beach. We suppressed our fear. We did not mention that topic.

The Israelis, however, were much ahead of us in this. Every time when a bomb exploded somewhere, or when someone was shot or stabbed, I was saying to myself: "Thank God, that nothing happened to *us*." Such attitude was alien to the Israelis. "One of *us* was hit again," they said. Soldiers were called "our children," the fellow countrymen and -women "*our people*," and the ones who fell in the war "our dead." And each one of these people lived with the awareness that soon he could be the next one.

I remember that on the day when the bomb in my son's school was detonated, his entire class, together with the teacher, visited us around noon, to see how he was. The kids did not say a word about what had happened in the school. Children, who could have been dead.

Next to the children, the second group of people that enjoyed special attention were the *olim*, the newcomers.

Rumor had it that the state received a certain amount of money from the United States as support for each *ole hadash,* or each newcomer. These funds were meant to secure housing in the *beth olim*, a stipend for the language course, health insurance, child support, and other social benefits. Another important aspect of the quick integration of immigrants was making sure that people did not stay unemployed forever. Thus, the Jewish Agency for Israel, the Sochnut, participated financially in the process of employing people. They sponsored a certain percentage of the labor costs of the employer. For many employers this was a strong motivation for hiring *olim*. Those who managed to get back on their feet quickly and wanted to purchase a home could also rely on generous loans. All of this was politics. What impressed me more than that was the relation of ordinary people toward immigrants.

...

When my son and I were *olim*, our friends took care of us in a fascinating way. Most of them were friends of my deceased uncle and knew each other. At some point they must have chosen their designated roles. Some of them would invite us frequently to their places so that we did not miss the atmosphere of a home. Others took care of arrangements with different government offices. Those who had more time were taking us out in order to show us the hidden beautiful corners of Tel Aviv. My friend from Jerusalem was taking care particularly of my son. He came from Jerusalem once every week to talk and to play with him, so that the boy did not miss a father figure completely.

Today, we still think often about Israel: About the terrace of our friend from Ramleh, where after the long hot days we had ice-coffee in the evening. We got to talk to her a lot about ourselves and she was listening with a kind of sympathy I had not seen before; she wanted to know everything, all the details, as if it was tremendously important to her to understand us and to be able to imagine everything we talked about. My entire past, my previous existence – they kept living in these conversations. I think that without this woman I might have lost myself. Friends who have sacrificed more time and energy for us than I have ever had for anyone else except for my children.

There were also strangers whom I will never forget.

One day we were shopping in Tel Aviv. A young woman heard us speak a foreign language. This is not unusual in Israel. At the register, however, she realized that we could not speak Ivrit at all. Then she asked in English where we were from, if we were *olim*, and since when we were *ba* aretz, at home in the country. In the afternoon on the same day, she appeared in front of our door in the asylum home with a huge linen sack full of clothes and toys for my boy. She did not come in. She was in a hurry. On the street outside there was a car with three children waiting for her. We never saw each other again.

Many schoolmates of my son were living in the same neighborhood. Often their mothers would take the Little One to their homes after school, so that he did not have to hang around in our little room all the time. Women whose names I did not even know.

...

I have always asked myself what it is that binds people in Israel to one another. This is a tiny little corner of the world where a stranger does matter to others. And, in my experience at the time, this fact had nothing to do with the famous Jewish solidarity. Perhaps it was life itself that was so precious to them.

Young Israelis, who had not been part of the pioneer times, were hearing from their parents how it was back then. In case there was no photograph of a family member fallen in a war in one's own home it could be certainly found in the home of the uncle or of the grandmother. Every family had to send their children – boys and girls – to the front. For going to the military in Israel meant going to the front. During the three years military service the families of soldiers lived as if they had cancer – they never knew if and for how long they would survive. Certainly, children were also brought up having that in mind. They grow up with the conviction that if they were not selfless and ready to sacrifice themselves their country would not survive even one more day. Those who are against this attitude leave the country. And if one wants to leave Israel, he/she is a disappointment to all who stay.

...

Once I visited my cousin in the desert Negev. He used to live in a moshav, a village, near the Dead Sea, together with his wife and two daughters. The moshav was newly developed. Its population consisted of young families that were engaged in agriculture and lived in tiny little concrete houses. At that point the whole settlement counted about fifty households. The houses were in the middle of the desert and they had no water supply yet. Water was delivered in canisters from far away. To protect their children against insects at night they had to cover their heads with insect net hats when they slept. No one was complaining about the conditions. They were talking a lot more about the pretty little gardens they were soon going to grow in front of their houses. I was eager to go with my cousin to his fields. We drove there around 4:30 one morning. My cousin was growing tomatoes in the middle of the desert. The beds were covered with plastic foil so that the plants did not burn in the heat. The irrigation was controlled by a computer. Very thin perforated plastic hoses were spread all over the ground. The water running through them could be absorbed into the soil only drop by drop. It was salt water from the Dead Sea. We had to go on with the work that had to be done there since, after 12 noon, the heat would have been unbearable. Around 11 I almost fainted. The temperature was about 50 degrees Celsius or 122 Fahrenheit. Hot air feels thick. It is as if one breathes in dense matter. There was no tree, no shelter, no place where one could hide in the shade. We left. On the backseat of the Jeep there was a machine gun. We were driving near the Jordanian border. In this area everyone who was going to the fields had to carry a weapon. It was impossible not to. Nothing else was possible. But people wanted to build something – from the nothingness around. I thought that in order to live there one needed to have a particular philosophy of life, a particular kind of consciousness. I think one needs them generally in order to live in Israel. People like the ones who lived in the moshav could never understand those who leave the country. The newcomers are considered by the Israelis *olim*, people who go up (to Israel), while the out-migrants are *yordim*, people who go down (from Israel).

I admired these people for their commitment, and I have to admit that I would not have had enough courage to live like that. I realized that it must be incredible to be building a country, but I was not convinced that I would be willing to participate in this regardless of the cost. I was not willing to take the responsibility for my sons, who someday, because of me, could have been sent to die unsuspectingly. I simply resisted the thought that war would be a permanent part of my life.

Other people, of course, could very well understand those who emigrated. They would have happily emigrated themselves if they had the opportunity. They were envious towards people whose lives were going to become easier and, sometimes, the envy even made such people malicious.

...

The worst experience I had in Israel was related to my decision to leave the country. Some friends were alienated and relatives were disappointed. The few people who were there for me even after I made my decision admitted that something between us had inevitably changed.

One day the wife of my late uncle organized a get-together with friends in her home. Among the guests were also the political emigrant from Bulgaria, whom I have previously mentioned, and his wife. As soon as we arrived in Israel, to be perfectly clear about everything, I had informed them about the report I had to write about them for the Bulgarian state security. They did not seem to be particularly surprised. However, when I tried to reach them later, their phone number was no longer in service.

When I asked common friends, I was told that it would be better to contact these people only through someone else and not directly. This sounded a bit awkward to me but I did not consider this fact very important. That evening, when we were all together in my aunt's house again, all of a sudden, they began some sort of a private interrogation. They wanted to know in the first place all details about my report and about the man who made me write about my previous visit to Israel. Unexpectedly, I was engaged in a conversation about my older son, though I could not figure out the connection to the state security questions.

It was no secret that I was calling my child once in a while. I wanted to hear his voice and to know how he was feeling. Most of all, I did not want him to doubt even for a moment that I was thinking of him all the time and wanted to make sure he knew that I had not abandoned him. At the same time, I also wanted to demonstrate clearly to anyone in Bulgaria who might have been intercepting our phone conversations that I had no intentions whatsoever to give up my son. I was always calling from different call boxes on the street. In case someone could figure out the number from which I was calling, that number could certainly not have been connected to my home address. Every time before I called, I had to think carefully how much information I could give my family and what kind of a code I could use to prevent giving away some secrets. Gradually, we established a whole complicated system of symbols and allusions in our conversations and we were very happy when we were able to decipher each other's thoughts.

In Bulgaria, there was an appalling way to deny one's parent or one's children formally through the State Newsletter. People had done this willingly or forcefully for different political reasons. Sadly, the son of the Bulgarian political emigrants had been pestered by the state security until he had done precisely that. Apparently, once he had even tried to lure his parents into a trap at the airport in Athens, on behalf of the state security. The parents were supposed to be killed there, but the attempted assassination failed. Somebody else showed up at the airport instead of them. This terrible experience had made my acquaintances very negative regarding any family relationships. They kept painting the devil on the wall. In their view, I had to give up the idea of a family reunion and I had to forget about my son in Bulgaria – forever, especially since I already had one child with me. In addition, I should not have counted on my husband's loyalty. According to them, he could easily be forced to cooperate with the state security in order to receive an exit permit himself. Their answer to my objection that I knew my husband well and that he was completely reliable was that they smiled with condescension. Gradually, this conversation became too uncanny for me. Across the table three grinning faces were staring at me. They talked on top of each other, and they were telling me stories about abandoned children and corrupted husbands. One more gruesome than the other. I could see only their mouths gaping open and noticed that the Little One, who had to listen to all this, had tears in his eyes. Suddenly, I slammed my fist on the table and said: "I will see my son again."

There was dead silence in the room.

"But of course," said the political emigrant writer's wife. "Obviously, she already has an agreement with the state security! How else could she be so sure?"

It was not only that these people did not want to see me ever again. They tried to discredit me in front of all friends and in front of the authorities. Their effort was not without consequences.

. . .

All the cost covered by the state for each immigrant counted in fact only as a loan. If one did not travel outside the country within the first five years, then the loan was forgiven. If, however, someone wanted to leave the country, for whatever reasons, then the loan had first to be repaid. Since it was possible to leave Israel only by plane, debts were saved in the airport computer system. There were many people who wanted to expatriate but had to work in the country for many years in order to collect the necessary money. When I decided to leave Israel, I did not owe astronomic amounts of money. Thus, I dared to ask my aunt, who had inherited a lot of money from my uncle, if she could lend me the amount of three thousand shekelim I needed. My aunt consulted the political emigrant couple.

It was not clear to me back then why these people were afraid mainly of the possibility that I might leave the country. I thought that, since they suspected me, it would have been much better for them if I disappeared. In any event, they advised my aunt not to give me the money so that I could not carry out my allegedly “mysterious” plan. It got even worse. Relatives in other Western countries were warned that most likely I had in mind a hellish plan. I never learned what precisely they had in mind.

Something almost no one wanted to believe was my honesty. My relatives had heard that I did not have a good marriage. Nobody believed that despite that, I did not wish to turn the father of my children into a scapegoat for the state security and that I felt an obligation to help him join us. They did not believe it especially because he was not Jewish.

“Get a divorce,” said an official once, “then we will see what we could do about your child.” The Mossad, the Israeli secret service, did not believe me either.

It is not unusual in Israel to call newcomers to the Mossad. When I escaped from Bulgaria, I thought that I would not have to deal with state security services ever again. But – no! I had to get to know the Israeli secret service too.

I had a conversation with two agents – according to the classic model which I already knew well. One of them was very rude, the other by contrast, quite understanding. One was trying to twist every single word in my mouth, while the other one was trying to calm me down. They started with Adam and Eve and continued up to the question of my intimate life.

“Did you have a romantic relationship with the man who gave you your passport the first time? Do you know that you are particularly dangerous because you are very intelligent? On top of this you speak several languages!”

I realized that I was stigmatized. In Bulgaria – because I had contacts to the West, and in the West because I came from Bulgaria. Would this curse follow me for the rest of my life?

However, over the course of this conversation it became clear that there was something else behind the whole story. The wife of the great political immigrant writer was afraid that I could kill her husband and then quickly disappear from the country. The Bulgarian government had ordered the murder of the writer Georgi Markov in London and was possibly involved in the assassination attempt on Pope John Paul II. Apparently, I might have been able to execute the next death sentence in absentia. Today I think that

I can understand these people. But back then, it was not very pleasant for me to realize that I was suspected.

Fortunately, the people from the Mossad had more sense than the Bulgarian immigrants. There is more that I have to admit. Their goal was not to scare people. Just the opposite. After they probably did a thorough check on me, they let me understand, in a very fine way, that I did not have to be afraid of anything anymore. Meanwhile, however, the Bulgarian secret service started chasing me.

In Bulgaria it was common for people to tell funny anecdotes. There were two famous joke figures with Armenian names and people really loved them. One of those anecdotes was about the secret agent Kirkor having to convey an important, top secret message to the secret agent Garabet. One evening, after he had finally found the secret place where Garabet was living in the West, Kirkor went there, very secretly. When he wanted to sneak into the building even more secretly, one of the Western residents of the same building tapped him on the shoulder and said:

"If you are looking for the secret agent Garabet, he lives on the third floor."

I do not wish to underestimate the qualities of the Bulgarian secret service. Nor can I swear that everything I thought was going on around me in Israel at the time was actually true. Nevertheless, I cannot resist the temptation to describe my perception.

It was common that in Israel immigrants who came from the same country would help each other. People in the *beth olim* exchanged experiences and gave each other advice. Any problem one had would be extensively discussed with others. Those who had already established some contacts and connections used to introduce the newcomers to people who, potentially, could help them. There was a nice young woman in our *beth olim* who had come to Israel in a remarkable way. She was very sweet and very honest, and we became friends. I was clear about the fact that my biggest problem was my older son with whom I wanted to be reunited as soon as possible. She felt for me and wanted to give me a tip on the possibilities. She told me that many years before her sister had emigrated from Bulgaria to Israel and was now married there. Thus, my friend, who had been left behind in Bulgaria, had no longer been able even to think about leaving the country. A member of her family revealed her true nature as a traitor to the republic and, consequently, the rest of the family had to pay for it. The parents died soon one after the other. My friend remained completely alone in the country. She was fired frequently from her jobs as a radiology technician. Every two, three years she had to move to a new city because of her new job. And every time she moved to another city, she tried to apply for official emigration, hoping that at some point it might work out. But in those days, there was no possibility for Jews to emigrate legally. Differently from many other people, this woman chose quite a direct approach. She wanted to renounce her Bulgarian citizenship officially. This complicated situation destroyed her life in Bulgaria almost completely. Emigrating became the only meaning of her existence and therefore she wanted to have no family of her own. When Yitzhak Shamir was elected prime minister of Israel, people learned that his wife was a Jew from Bulgaria. My friend's sister wrote to Mrs. Shamir and eventually she was invited to an audience.

Diplomatic relations between Israel and Bulgaria had been broken in 1968, so in the mid-1980s Mrs. Shamir came to Bulgaria as the very first political person to visit the country, following a private invitation issued by the wife of the foreign minister, Petâr Mladenov. Bulgaria did not make a big deal out of it. There was only a small spectacle, staged in the Synagogue, that had been "closed for renovations" for years. The young rabbi let a beard grow and finally held a service, behind closed doors. Just in case, the service was filmed for the historical archive. Naturally, the two important ladies discussed some private issues, as was common at such quasi-private events. Mrs. Shamir, who had taken the problem of my friend to heart, talked about it openly to Mrs. Mladenov. One evening, soon after this conversation, two agents of the state security came to the young woman's home, quietly and secretly. They put a passport with a tourist visa for Israel in her hand. She had to leave the country in a hush-hush operation, within eight hours and without saying goodbye to anyone.

After I heard this story, I put all my hopes for a family reunion on Mrs. Shamir. I found a contact to her, though it was only indirect. However, she was not willing to do anything about it. She was afraid that if she used political connections for personal reasons, she could ruin her husband's reputation.

It was simply the wrong time. Bulgaria was just considering whether diplomatic relations with Israel should be reestablished or not. Apparently, the two countries were in the process of unofficial negotiations and I was simply unfortunate.

The woman who had come to Israel with the help of Mrs. Shamir introduced me to a young family from Bulgaria. They started inviting us to visit them frequently and apparently wanted to help us. It was quite cozy to get together with them in their wonderful apartment once in a while. The husband was particularly intelligent and a nice conversational partner. However, there was something that bothered me from the very beginning. I knew that the father of this nice man was a well-known statesman in Bulgaria and that he belonged to the entourage of Todor Zhivkov as his political advisor. Before he came to Israel, the son had been working for the Bulgarian embassies in different countries. He insisted that he always wanted to be free of the *nomenclatura* and to immigrate to Israel. His wife, who was not Jewish, hated Israel and the Israelis, and did not want to hear anything about learning the language. Thanks to her knowledge of English, she was working for an American company and managed to live absolutely isolated in her apartment, furnished in a "European" style. Soon I realized that these people were extremely interested in a few particular questions: how we escaped from Bulgaria, who helped us, and most of all, what we intended to do and on whom we could rely in Israel. I was always very careful but rejected the idea that our new acquaintances were asking such questions for reasons other than pure curiosity. Until one time they organized a very special dinner. I had never stood in front of a judge but now I had the feeling that I had to justify myself because of some crime I had committed.

Concerning my escape, I had a few good stories ready. I was concerned about my husband and my older son whom I had left behind. I had no idea in what way they might be harassed. The more upset the authorities became with the absconder, the higher the price her/his relatives had to pay. So, I downplayed the official version of my escape, out of concern for my family in Bulgaria. To people I did not know well, particularly to Bulgarians, I was explaining that my younger son had a heart disease and that I wanted him to be treated in the West. Nevertheless, I also made it clear that I was terribly concerned about my older son. People who did not know me could have thought that I was simply a confused woman, who had escaped because she was desperately afraid about the illness of her child. My new acquaintances thought they could influence me and convince me to go back to Bulgaria, for otherwise "I would never see my other son again."

The very intelligent diplomat offered, in very clear terms, to call his father in Sofia and to ask him to help me do this. Apparently, he could have guaranteed impunity from prosecution and, thus, I would have no reason to be afraid. However, I was able to put all the links together only when this man asked me whether, by any chance, I had access to the State Archive while I was working as language instructor at the department of history at the University. The political immigrant I have mentioned many times was a historian and had published several books about Bulgaria under communism from the perspective of a regime opponent. Since I had left in a mad rush and completely unexpectedly, the authorities must have imagined that I had taken along top-secret documents on behalf of their famous opponent.

I put an end to the discussion by telling the diplomat very clearly that I had no intentions to go back to Bulgaria. He realized that I wasn't born yesterday as it had seemed to him initially. He tried a few more times to squeeze out something from both my son and me but his efforts were to no avail. I never understood why this was so important to him, but he tried very hard to figure out whether we intended to move to Germany. He even offered to take me to the German embassy and to help me ask for advice regarding my potential immigration to Germany. Every now and then he would show up in our *beth olim* to take my son for a walk or to invite him to ice cream. I never took the bait. Once, my son was alone at home. The diplomat showed up again. He suggested that the two of them go for ice cream. My son did go. They bought ice cream, they played a game, and they looked at toy cars in the window of a shop. And then, out of the blue, the diplomat sked:

"Have you been already in the German embassy with your mother?"

"I can't remember," said my son. "Why don't you ask my Mom?"

Soon after, when this man and I spoke to each other for the last time, he admitted that he had underestimated us.

...

The other Bulgarian who appeared around us was not so intelligent. A few months after we arrived in Israel someone called me in the *beth olim*. He said that he received my phone number from my aunt and that he absolutely had to see me. It was impossible for this man to explain who exactly this alleged aunt was, but I accepted to see him. We met in the foyer of the asylum home. The man had just arrived from Bulgaria, together with his little boy. He was visiting relatives in Tel Aviv and wanted my opinion of the question whether he should stay in Israel with his son or not. I was supposed to explain to him how exactly everything worked and to tell him what I was satisfied with and what I did not like. I refused to give him such advice, but he did not want to give up. He tried to provoke me with all sorts of questions. After a long conversation which was supposed to help him make his decision, he admitted that he was flying back to Bulgaria in two days and that, actually, he had no intentions to live in Israel. I was not able to figure out if this open confession that he wanted only to pick my brains was deliberate or just stupid.

With time, I got used to such attempts to intervene in my decisions. Every time something similar happened, I was left with a bitter aftertaste. I knew that I was followed and observed, but gradually I learned not to agonize about it. Instead, I was turning toward the more concrete task of surviving.

Surviving was no longer an easy task for us.

I realized that one year after their arrival all immigrants and their under-age children received Israeli citizenship automatically. At the time I was not at all certain that, given the circumstances, I really wanted it. Morally, I was not prepared to make this decision for my sons. In addition, being based in Israel I could not do anything about a family reunion and I just did not know what to do. I discussed all this very openly with the authorities and wanted to reject the citizenship. I must say that my wish was respected in a very fair manner, though perhaps with some intervention from a few friends. Immediately after I applied for the rejection of Israeli citizenship in writing, many of the social benefits we received from the state were cut – something that made sense to me. However, we were allowed to keep living in the *beth olim* and my stipend for the language course was not taken away either. In other words, we were not put on the street. Nevertheless, I no longer had the right to receive child support or any other subsidies, and I had to take over paying my health insurance. There followed a period of time when every evening I doubted that I would be able to buy food on the next day. I started looking for a job. The quickest way to make some money was to clean other people's houses. Since initially I did not see many other options, I decided to distribute an announcement in the neighborhood. This emergency situation was certainly a low point in my life, but I cannot say that I really suffered. I tried to look at all this as experience and thought that "having to clean had some heroic aspect." I was convinced that it would only make me stronger. Armed with this attitude I started working in the homes of strangers.

Usually, I was working in the morning. If someone asked me to go in the afternoon, however, the Little One was resolved that he should come along. I was cleaning and, meanwhile, he was sitting in some corner doing his homework. Despite my positive attitude, at the end of my working day I was always feeling a bit depressed. My boy always tried to cheer me up. Once, we were together in somebody's place again. The owners were very demanding and wanted me to polish their mahogany furniture every time I cleaned. I am relatively short and I must have looked very funny – standing on the ladder, stretching my hands and not being able to reach the top shelf of the book case. The Little One was looking at me. Suddenly he said:

"You clean very well Mom!"

However, soon I had to put an end to this occupation.

One morning I was in the mahogany place again. Alone. The father of the family was at home alone too. I was dusting the bookshelves thoroughly. Suddenly, the guy asked if I would like a cup of coffee. "Yes, please," I said and kept dusting. A few minutes later he came back to the living room, carrying a silver tray with two cups of nice Chinese porcelain on it. He was naked. I did not move from the ladder. He waited. Eventually, I told him to put my coffee on the table – I was going to have it later. He sat down slowly in his armchair, leaned back, and kept staring at me. Another half an hour

In the Beth Olim

passed and I could not come up with any better idea than to keep cleaning. Then I heard how he locked the entrance door. He ordered me to clean the bathtub. I refused and said that I had to finish cleaning the windows. I climbed to the top of the ladder and opened the window. The apartment was on the fourth floor and I got dizzy looking down. The guy wouldn't stop. He wanted to get me in the bathroom. I threatened that if he came near me, I would jump from the window. He remained in the living room and stretched on the sofa. I did not see a way out. At some point he went to the toilet. I jumped down from the ladder and dialed the phone number of friends who lived nearby. I managed to tell them only the address and the name of my employer before I had to hang up because I heard him coming back. Five minutes later the doorbell rang. He was surprised. I said, someone was coming for me. He threw the keys on the table and ran into the bedroom to get dressed. When I saw my friends at the door, I just wanted to leave and did not say a word about what happened. The owner of the mahogany place paid me and gave me five shekelim more than agreed. This must have been the price for my silence.

This was the end of my cleaning career and of my attitude toward accepting any honorable job. My Romanian neighbor in the *beth olim* helped me get part time teaching contracts at the Goethe Institute and at a private language school. There was also a lot of work for translators and we were able to keep our heads above water.

Birthday celebration

Menorah and Candelabra

One day my son came home from school and asked me what a *goy* was. The other boys in his class had realized that he wasn't circumcised, and that he was thus an unbeliever. There were many immigrant families from countries of the former Eastern Bloc where a circumcision would have been impossible, even forbidden. Many of the parents had their boys circumcised in Israel as a gesture of their fundamentally patriotic attitude but disregarding the age of their children. In my circle of acquaintances in Tel Aviv I saw boys of various ages running around with legs spread unnaturally far from one another. Often, they were in so much pain that they could barely go to the toilet. I had nothing against circumcision. I could also imagine that there were people who, out of their deep religious beliefs, were willing to circumcise their children even in a later age. Some of the parents, however, did this only in order to be liked by the Orthodox Jews. The more strictly a family observed the Jewish customs and traditions, the more they stuck to kosher food, the bigger was their chance to be supported – financially, socially, and professionally. I had a lot of respect for people's religious views. However, the way some were misusing the notion of Jewishness was out of proportion; particularly the legendary fact that Jews support each other. I knew faithful Jews and I knew pretenders, and it was not a big science to tell them apart. There were also those who were trying to delude others as well as themselves, just in order to receive housing or a stipend for the better education of their children. Apparently, this was not happening only in Israel. I heard that one of my former Bulgarian colleagues, who was of a purely Bulgarian origin, fled the country and settled in London. She then let her son be circumcised at the age of fifteen, simply because she did not find any other college sponsor but the Synagogue. She even dyed her blond hair red and started to asseverate her "true" Jewish religion. Another woman I knew supplied herself with a small silver star of David. She would wear it on a chain, like a necklace, every time when she went to meetings in a certain Jewish organization, in order to negotiate about the possibilities of financing her dissertation that was related to the Jewry in Eastern Europe.

Personally, I had no desire to prove anything to anyone. I wanted my children and me to remain exactly what we had always been. I felt very comfortable in my mixed-blood skin and I wanted to bring up my children in a way that would allow them to feel comfortable with that too.

It was not at all easy to explain to my son what the word *goy* meant. The child was confused. He was not treated badly by the other children in any way. Quite the opposite. He had friends with whom he was spending a lot of time. He was just different. He was different in the same way in which I was different in Bulgaria. Did he have to suffer as I had suffered?

I myself became "different" in Israel again.

In Bulgaria people thought of me as Judith the Jew. However, according to the Jewish law, I was no Jew, because my mother wasn't Jewish. I had the Biblical "right of return" to Israel, but frequently people said to me:

"Oh, of course, you are actually only half... "

I was neither fish nor fowl. I realized that I was developing very strange feelings. Before, I always had to defend my Jewish half. I protected it and I nourished it and with time it was becoming more and more important to me. I tried to learn a little bit of Hebrew and I tried to organize at least a Passover celebration in a very small circle of close friends.

For many years my father had avoided celebrating Passover. I believed that he was not religious at all and that he had almost no knowledge of the Jewish traditions. When I showed some interest, however, it turned out that he was quite capable of organizing a real Jewish family celebration. He read from the Torah, and did everything appropriately, according to tradition. I was fifteen when we celebrated Passover at home for the first time. And I figured that I did not know the first thing yet about my father.

During the Holocaust my father was sent to a forced labor camp for Jews near the Bulgarian town of Cherven Bryag at the Danube. This must have been terrible, nevertheless it was not a death camp like those where most of his relatives perished in the gas chambers. In fact, saving the Bulgarian Jews from deportation was due to a high degree to the personal intervention of Tsar Boris III. Apparently, Hitler had him poisoned, most likely because of the Tsar's political stubbornness. The movement against fascism in Bulgaria was closely related to the communist movement. Thus, many Jews became members of the communist party and participated in the coup of 1944 in one way or another. After the coup most of the Jews appeared to be complaisant toward the new regime, for they had been spared the gas chambers due to the very specific political circumstances in Bulgaria, including the existence of the communist movement. They were trying to be loyal citizens and to live in agreement with the law and the society. That also required them to suppress the forbidden religious feelings of a Jew. The same applied to my father.

Back then, he celebrated Passover at my wish for the first time in years, together with his family and a few young Jewish friends, whom I invited. He rose from his place of honor at the end of the long dining table, his kippah on his head, in order to read from the Torah. His otherwise sad eyes were glowing and he was happy, for he could be himself again. His eyes had the expression of his profound love for the history and the tradition of his people, an expression of love that had been denied him over decades again and again. First by the Nazis and then by the communists.

At that Seder he gave me as a gift the yellow Jewish star that he had to wear under the Nazis. At the same time, he also gave me his blessing – something that according to Jewish tradition is reserved only for the first-born son.

...

It was a few days before Christmas. My son asked when we would get a Christmas tree. I tried to explain to him that there were no Christmas trees in Israel. He looked surprised. I also explained to him why Christmas was not celebrated there. To no avail. In the first eight years of his life we always managed to have a big Christmas celebration, even though this was forbidden in Bulgaria. His father, who was Christian, always wanted to invite someone who was alone and had no family to Christmas Eve. Every year, the children wrote letters to Santa and prepared a whole repertoire of songs and poems to perform in front of him. Then Santa came unfailingly, just before Christmas Eve began, a huge linen bag on his shoulders, in a genuine red robe, with a long white beard, and he brought them presents.

When I tried to explain to my son that, now, we could not celebrate Christmas, he looked at me with astonishment and asked:

"What kind of a country is this, where Santa does not come?"

I put him on my lap and told him the sad story about the invented Santa. I told him who lent us the red robe every year and who played Santa. I quoted each single conversation he had with the false Santa and I reminded him of all the songs he sang to him. Eventually, I wanted to see if he understood all this and he said "yes." He stared for a while at the distance and then he asked:

"And who does the real Santa go to?"

After I had protected my Jewish half from myself and from others for over thirty years, now I felt the need to protect my other half of my mixed-blood existence. I wanted to celebrate Christmas again.

Many times I have asked myself if it is necessary for every human being to belong to something. Sometimes I felt guilty towards my father because I could not identify myself with Judaism one hundred percent. Every now and then I had also doubts that, in my case, Christian philosophy, that meant a lot to me, might not have been as genuine as in the case of someone who was brought up only as a Christian. Nevertheless, I have never had any identity crisis. Perhaps because I had faith in God and my religious attitude was becoming ever stronger. I discovered that I did not have to choose one religion, one culture, one part of myself. To acknowledge my deep connection to Judaism and at the same time to pledge myself to Christianity was something natural and self-evident. Denying one of them would have meant to me denying God.

I shared my son's concern about not going to see Santa this year with my neighbor, a woman from Romania who lived in the room next to us. She liked my son very much and tried to help us, most of all because of him. She called friends who, as far as she knew, did celebrate Christmas, and she asked them to invite me and my son. We went to their place. For my son, this was the last Christmas he celebrated with Santa. This was how, accidentally, we became involved with Christians in Israel.

The life of Christians in Israel seemed to be different from that in a Christian country. There are Christian missions in Israel in which a real missionary spirit is predominant. The state tolerated priests and believers, but there were many reservations against them. Frequently, people who worked in a mission were considered to be spies or provocateurs. Some of them may well have been exactly that. Nevertheless, there was a certain sense of early

Christianity that could make their lives there quite fascinating – especially if one did not know the background. And the background involved all sorts of political, clerical, and even personal peculiarities. The common attitude of Christian clerics sent to the missions was that they should respect the state of Israel which, however, does not have the blessing of Christ. This fact, in their view, had turned the country into a goddamn spot on earth, where people had to make endless sacrifices as a punishment for their great sin – the betrayal of Jesus. As good Christians they accepted the idea of the Old Testament that the Jews were the chosen people, but they were convinced that the Israelis had nothing to do with the Biblical Hebrews. Thus, eventually, Jews had to be converted in order to be released from the curse of history. Each conversion was seen as a major success in the work of the particular mission and was attributed to the priest of the respective parish. However, it was not clear to anyone what exactly Yahweh and Jesus had to do with the cloud of lead hanging over Israel.

We met priests who were pure in heart and were doing their job with clear conscience, and we met others who looked at their time in Israel as if it were a punishment. Often, family members of Christian priests hated that country so much that they preferred to hide behind the walls of the missionary houses, and they were not interested in any contact with the Israelis. Thus, their life there would turn into an unbearable waiting for their missionary mandate to expire.

At the same time, missions were terribly misused by immigrants. The Christian missions in Israel were as attractive to refugees and settlers as were the synagogues in Europe. No doubt that many mixed Christian-Jewish families were coming to Israel and that sometimes one of the partners, based on his or her Christian upbringing, felt inclined to join one or the other church. There were also immigrants, such as myself, who were children of mixed families. Some of them realized only when they arrived in Israel that they had to choose one of the two sides of their previous existence. However, there were also plenty of people to whom belonging to a Christian community meant simply having a lavish Sunday breakfast in the community house after the service. Alternatively, it could have also meant having a big station wagon at their disposal, provided they demonstrated active participation in the community life. Such people pretended to have faith, they falsified certificates of baptism and told all sorts of made-up stories which the priests were under pressure to believe.

In the beginning, I did not know the background yet. We ended up in an Evangelical-Lutheran community in Jaffa that appeared to be a beautiful oasis in the spiritual life of immigrants. At a certain point, I had joined an Evangelical-Lutheran community already in Sofia. Rather, I often went to the service they had. Toward the end of the 1960s my sister and I by chance met a young organ player. Originally, he had studied chemistry in Sofia. Later, he was accepted at the Dresden Conservatory and, with great difficulties, was allowed by the Bulgarian authorities to study organ there. He was a born musician and could live really only through his music, and soon he became a member of the international Bach Society. For about half a year before we met him he had been fighting with the authorities for the extension of his travel permit. The authorities must have considered him to be suspicious because in addition to being some kind of an artist, he was also Evangelical-Lutheran, and he played the organ. Organ was not among the instruments taught in the Bulgarian conservatories which, otherwise, had a very good reputation in Europe. The choral music of the Orthodox Church could still be put somehow into the common denominator "national tradition." Since organ, however, did not belong in the Orthodox Church, organ music counted exclusively as part of Western European religious tradition. Consequently, as an instrument organ was accepted neither in the church nor in the concert hall – for it was a device of Western influence. There was a famous old organ in the Catholic church in Russe, a city at the Danube. Its sound had been long forgotten. In Russe, there was a small Catholic community. They were allowed to have their service in the church, nevertheless they were strictly forbidden to play the organ. Eventually, in the 1970s the minister of culture Liudmila Zhivkova, the daughter of the prime minister Todor Zhivkov, ordered the first concert organ to be built in the biggest hall at the time, *Bulgaria.*

Our friend, who at the end of the 1960s was fighting for a permission to go back to Dresden, was looking for an opportunity to practice his music in Sofia. He learned that the Evangelical-Lutheran church had a small harmonium. He started playing there regularly during the service and eventually invited us to join him from time to time. This is how we came to this church. Our communication to this person was remarkable. We listened to organ music together and he would tell us about great organ performers, about the Bach Society, and about the concerts in the churches of Dresden. He could barely discuss any other topic – not because he was ignorant but because music filled every single moment of his life. This friendship meant a lot to us since both my sister and I were musicians – I was at the music high school at the time and she was at the conservatory. Similarly to our friend, we also lived almost only through our music. The evenings all three of us spent together were rare escapes from our daily life into a spiritual world which we slowly entered led by the young man.

He did not receive a travel permit. His parents insisted that he continue his study of chemistry in Sofia. There was no organ yet anywhere on the Bulgarian horizon. One evening his father found him in the attic. He had hanged himself. He was still warm. The father tried to give him CPR, without realizing in the dark that this was his own son.

On the day after the funeral the travel permit arrived. No one believed that he would have received it if he had been alive. The authorities wanted just to wash their hands from the guilt because the young man was a member of a big international organization, the Bach Society.

This friendship and the fact that Dânov, the founder of the *Brotherhood of Light*, had switched from the Orthodox to the Evangelical-Lutheran Church made me think that, at the time, the Evangelical-Lutheran churches in Europe might have been the most tolerant ones.[10] My opinion was supported also by the accidental discovery of the Evangelical-Lutheran parish in Israel.

This was a Norwegian mission. Due to his fascinating and unusual attitudes the pastor, who was of noble Spanish descent, had a very strong impact on the entire atmosphere of the church. In his "temple of faith," as he called his church, there was nothing to remind people of punishment, suffering, and martyrdom. Not even the crucifix was there. The Saturday services there were always dominated by an incomparably inspiring mood. This was not so much due to the pastor's preaching as to the way he was

---

[10] At the time I had knowledge neither of the Bible Belt in North America nor of the negative aspects in the history of European Protestantism.

praying. In addition to some hymns, people sang songs accompanied by guitar, tambourine, or by whatever other instrument any parishioner could play. This church was against exaltations and possible visions seen in trance. People were praying in a very normal way and with ardor – some aloud and some in silence – each in their own language. When someone was praying aloud, most other people were praying with and for him/her. Often, it was as if a powerful energy field was created that was almost tangible. As if the people there were joining some colossal link of love, faith, and hope.

...

One day the pastor gave us time to pray again. Everybody was still sitting quietly. Suddenly, I heard my son pray. In Bulgarian. He was praying about his brother and his father, and about all of us being reunited again; he was praying for strength and for hope, and he gave thanks – again and again.

That day, for the first time, the pastor gave him the Holy Communion. The boy was eight. Later, some people asked why. The pastor said that one should receive the Holy Communion when he/she is able to recognize God. This child, according to him, was ready for that. Age, he said, had nothing to do with it.

Numbered People

My son and I spent a lot of time with the pastor, his wife, and his children. Every Saturday afternoon, after the service, they took us to their home and we often traveled with them through the country. My son felt safe in their home. The whole family loved him. The time we had together was never enough for our profound discussions about all possible subjects. Our conversations left a strong imprint on my outlook. The friendship we developed reached beyond the obligations of a church pastor. Today, I know that heroes and fairy tale princes are human beings of flesh and blood like us, and that they could be way more fascinating in real life than in the most wonderful dream. However, frequently, we look through them without seeing them, because we ourselves are blind.

Nevertheless, soon I realized that even his community had its problems. There too people fought and schemed against each other.

My neighbor from Romania, who was generally an atheist and a skeptic, tried to convince me that the character of this community, including my friendship with the pastor, had a purely political background. In her opinion, "no one really gave a damn about the fate of others," because everyone was only a sheer number for everybody else. Help, moral support, friendship – all good things that surrounded me, were to be seen only in the context of the complex political and ideological goals that people pursued in that country. This woman was to me something like my inner voice that brought me back to reality. Over the course of many months, she always managed to subdue my idealism and to help me get down to earth again. Even though I resisted accepting her view of the number-person, my trusting nature was partly shaken, and I was quite close to feeling like a sheer number myself.

In Israel, it was very difficult for me to deal with the sandy wind *khamsin.* I was often short of breath and dizzy. One evening I was feeling very miserable. I had no sense of balance and could not stand on my feet. By chance, the daughter of the pastor stopped by to invite my son to play with her siblings. She found me in a desperate condition. Half an hour later, her father came. At that point, I no longer had health insurance. The pastor brought me to a private hospital where they did all possible tests and where they treated me. After we left the hospital, he took me and my son for a few days to his home. His wife took care of me. I was not feeling comfortable and did not want to be a burden to them. Thus, I repeatedly tried to convince them to let me go home. The pastor said once with surprise:

"Why can you not accept help? You are not some number but a human being, and we love you!"

. . .

Most people think that there are no miracles. However, many of the experiences my son and I had in the first year after we left Bulgaria verged on miraculous reality or real miracles.

When I was little, I loved best the fairy tales of Wilhelm Hauff. My favorite character was Sandmännchen (Sandman). I always wished that someday he would get me out of a jam, using his magic wand.

Since there were no diplomatic relations with Bulgaria, there was no formal way for me to apply for family reunion while I was living in Israel. Friends were telling me that if I were in Germany, I would have a bigger chance to see my older son sooner rather than later. I had already wanted to go to Germany before, but I was sent away by the German officials in Belgrade. When I went to the German Embassy in Tel Aviv for the first time, I had no idea that I had the right to German citizenship because I was of German descent. After I had given up my previous life, I accepted the fact that it might take a very long time before I would belong anywhere in the world again. In the embassy, I was received by a young man who was not in a hurry and who listened to me. By contrast to many other ethnic Germans who, as I realized later, came to the embassy with all sorts of demands, I had no idea what I could ask for, and what I could expect. While I was talking, the young man was looking straight in my eyes – very seriously but with a gentle look. Unlike his colleagues in Belgrade, he did not withhold from me what I had the right to know. Namely, that as an ethnic German I had the right to the German citizenship. He explained my case to me exactly and what the possibilities were to move to Germany. Over the course of the next nine months he discussed every single decision with me – step by step. I would have never achieved what I am and what I have today, without the advice of this man. He helped me out of pure compassion, without ever taking any advantage of my situation or overstepping his professional obligations. Only after I became a German citizen and had all my papers did we become friends. Until today, his wife and he are among my most beloved friends. We have always kept in touch. When I was already living in Germany and they were still in Israel, we saw each other every time they came home. Often we travelled many kilometers in order to see each other. If I had a problem, I always called them. In the beginning of my life in Germany I did not take any important step without first consulting them. At a point when I was absolutely on my own and had, yet again, to pack my stuff and move to Germany, to another foreign country, this man said to me:

"Don't be afraid. We will manage."

I had not heard this magic Plural form since my father died and I never forgot it. Later, in a letter, my friend wrote me:

"I have also seen us all sitting in a boat together and wanting to reach a common goal. This is how I view helping you and you do not need to thank me all the time."

Shortly after I arrived in Germany, a clerk in one of the immigration offices, a lady, tried to wise me up by telling me that some "big fish has intervened with the authorities" on my behalf, in order to speed up the process of my naturalization. She told me absolutely blatantly that I must have had a relationship with that person. The Bulgarian State Security, the Israeli secret service, and now the German authorities. It was all the same. Why did everybody think of a romantic relationship? Because I was a young woman? On top of this, I had no clue to whom I was supposed to be grateful. There were a few people who might have come through for me. Apparently, none of them wanted me to feel obliged.

"What does friendship actually mean?" one of my German colleagues once asked me. "I think this is a socialist notion that you have grown up with. Who has real friends nowadays anyway?"

I had a few, I thought. I had experienced friendship at first hand.

...

In order to leave Israel, first I had to pay back my debts to the state. Things looked pretty hopeless for me. If I wanted to make the money I needed on my own, I would have had to remain for many more years in the country.

Only one of all my friends who knew about this problem offered to help me with two hundred shekelim. I was never able to beg and to go from door to door. Sometimes in the evening, after my boy went to bed, I spent hours sitting on the terrace and staring in the distance – until I was so tired that I would fall asleep in the fresh cool air. Why aren't there real miracles, I thought to myself. Why couldn't some wonderful person come to me and offer to lend me the money? It was so nice and so comforting just to think about the possibility, even if only for an instant. But the wonderful person came indeed. One evening he appeared at my door with a bouquet of red roses in his hand. He came in quietly and said:

"I waited for a long time for you to ask me for help, but you did not. Thus, I would like to offer you my help. Take the money that you need from me. I am not giving it to you as a gift. I trust, someday, you will pay me back."

This man had known me just for a few months and the only thing he knew about me with certainly was that I wanted to go out into the world. His trust meant more to me than any kind of alms that others might have offered.

...

My son and I were going to take yet another plane. In only a few hours we were going to lose a whole world, that was supposed to be replaced by the uncertainty of a far-away place. The night before we left Tel Aviv our friends from the German embassy took us for a last drive through the city we were parting with. We stopped for the last time at the Shuk Ha'Carmel, the big marketplace with colorful wheelbarrows full of delicacies, where old Jews in kippah and barefoot Arab children advertised their goods by crying out loud and making witty jokes. Textiles with all colors of the rainbow, exotic fruit, fresh fish and oriental sweets, Persian carpets and Israeli bananas peeped at the heat from under the linen canopies. They enticed us into that unreal fairy tale world, where one could expect the Caliph Stork to appear on a flying carpet just about any minute. Alternatively, one could also expect that at the next corner, for one reason or another, someone could be killed

We said goodbye to a world we loved and we feared.

It was June. Tel Aviv, the City of Spring, smelled intoxicatingly of jasmine.

"*L'shanah haba'ah ba Yerushalayim*. Next Year in Jerusalem," say Jews in the Diaspora when they toast at Rosh Hashanah, while at the same time they make plans of the future in which nowadays Israel often has a place only in their hearts.

"Stock und Hut"[11]

"Why don't you go home?" asked a colleague of mine when my teaching contract in Germany expired and I became unemployed.

I had lived in Germany for five years. Munich had become my home and every time after I had travelled abroad, I looked forward to coming back. Germany had been for me the country of Goethe, Thomas Mann, and Feuchtwanger, of Borchert and the Grimm Brothers, and sharing this country with them was something that made me extremely happy.

"I have to warn you," said my friend, the professor from Bremen, when we saw each other for the first time after I arrived, "this is not the land of poets and thinkers that you have probably dreamed of."

Initially my son and I settled in a small town in Northern Germany. Immediately I had to start dealing with the authorities. I had the naïve idea that in the free world people would be glad for everyone who has been able to achieve their freedom. I believe that up until the political changes in Eastern Europe, people kept coming to the West hoping that they would be received with admiration and that they would hear words such as "Look at them, they have really managed! Good for them. Let us help them and support them now!" However, a few events which shook up my idealism profoundly helped me sober up and gain back my sense of reality.

Two weeks after we arrived I started looking for a job. First, I called a professor whose name I had heard already in Bulgaria. I knew that he was working in the area of Bulgarian studies and that he was teaching Bulgarian language, literature, and history, at a particular university. I wanted simply to ask him how to approach looking for a teaching position. I told him who I was, how I knew his name, what I had accomplished in the fields of German and Slavic studies and who could give him references about me.

"How exactly do you imagine this?" he yelled at me. "Do you think that you could show up here and that anyone would hire you without letting people in Sofia know about that?"

---

[11] German for "Hat and Stick." A verse from the German folk song *Hänschen Klein* (Little Hans). The original words are symbolic for the little boy who packs his things and ventures to the world.

Later, when I was working as a Lecturer at the University of Munich, I learned that in the former West Germany there were two types of lectureships in Bulgarian studies: The so called "official lectureships" and the "other ones." The guardians of the "official lectureships" maintained friendly relationships with Bulgaria and hired only lecturers who were sent or recommended by their colleagues in Sofia. At the same time, the German professors who worked in the field were constantly invited to conferences and seminars in Sofia. Their research was funded by the "Center for Bulgarian Studies" and they were offered free vacation housing at the Black Sea coast. I figured that a certain kind of a holiday scholarship had developed and that it had partly affected the character of Bulgarian studies in Germany. This is why there were for example some talks and publications that represented typically communist interpretations of literature and aesthetics.

By contrast, the "other" Bulgarian lectureships were known as "independent." In these cases, it was the university that chose who should be invited to give a talk. Those institutions were particularly interested in offering a forum to scholars who were repressed or underestimated in Bulgaria and other socialist countries. To Bulgaria, though, the scholarship that came out of those universities was provocative and hostile. The Bulgarian state saw the development of Bulgaria studies abroad as extremely important. Thus, the government in Sofia was focused on occupying teaching positions particularly at those "independent" Slavic departments. The goal was to create more and more bastions of the communist political ideology.

...

In the aftermath of Perestroika, many organizations tried to gain a foothold in Eastern European countries too. The Bavarian Jugendring (Youth Ring), an association of many German youth organizations, established contacts to the Bulgarian Komsomol, the only youth organization in Bulgaria at the time. They wanted to develop some program for cooperation. Bavaria invited secretaries of local Komsomol units in the city of Gabrovo. They came as representatives of the youth organizations in the region, in order to negotiate and sign different agreements. The Jugendring needed an interpreter and I needed money. The idea was explained to me in detail and I accepted to be available for ten days.

In those days I was trying to avoid contacts to Bulgarians as much as possible. Therefore, I did not like telling Bulgarians my name or where I was working. But the representative of the Jugendring, who was in charge of welcoming the delegation and of showing them Bavaria, was a lot more concerned than me. She was afraid that the association could discredit itself in the eyes of the Bulgarians if they discovered that the Bavarians had hired a fresh Bulgarian refugee to work for them. In Germany, a country where everybody says his last name even when they answer the phone, I had to be constantly introduced as "the interpreter" to mayors, businessmen, and all sorts of party activists, and I had to play dumb when someone asked for my name. When I got sick of these secrecy games and started introducing myself with my last name, the lady was very upset.

On the whole, the ten days I spent working with the Bulgarian delegation on behalf of the Bavarian Jugendring reminded me of the way agreements and contracts were signed with representatives of the Western world in Bulgaria, namely in the evening, after the official schedule for the day, after one had already had a few drinks.

I had often asked myself before, how was it that every now and then prominent personalities from the Western World, particularly Europe, showed quite some sympathy for the Bulgarian government. According to people who worked as interpreters for the government in Bulgaria, negotiations about many decisions that had to be made together with representatives of the Western world were conducted on a very personal level. Apparently, this did not affect big politics, but it was possible to imagine how it might happen. Over four decades, the things that were so attractive in Bulgaria to Western scholars and statesmen and –women, were, among others, the Black Sea coast and the free vacation in recreational homes and resorts owned by the communist party. In addition to the many so called "residences" of the government, in fact converted palaces from before the coup, the administration of each single party organization had bigger or smaller recreational homes in the mountains and at the Black Sea coast. There, the government used to offer lavish feasts for local functionaries as well as for guests from the West. At a time when a normal mortal Bulgarian had to stand for very long time in line for milk and when mothers who could not breastfeed their children could not afford to buy

Formula for their babies, those who belonged to the crème-de-la-crème of the communist society were served the most exotic titbits, delivered from special stores called "diplomatic stores." If a person of high stature was concerned, such as Franz-Joseph Strauss[12] for example, then the authorities organized in addition a government hunt too. I heard a funny story from a classmate of mine who used to work frequently as an interpreter for German politicians. The Bulgarian government was so eager to please its Western guests that it took its hunting tasks very seriously. Apparently, they would sometimes let trained animals, which had been given alcoholic drinks, run in front of the diplomatic shotguns, so that the guests could not miss them. Once, an English Lord discovered this clever trick by the smell when he was skinning the animal and reported about this in a small local newspaper in England.

On another occasion, when I was visiting friends one evening in the very first few months after my arrival, I came to realize that no one in Germany would applaud me for having come to the homeland of my ancestors. It was the second time my son and I were invited by these people. The business partner of our host was also there. We were having a very pleasant conversation. It turned out that the other guest had been once in Sofia on a business trip. He was telling us about the places he still remembered. Among others, he mentioned that he had seen the big mosque with the golden onion domes too. I corrected him, explaining that the mosque he was talking about was actually an Orthodox church. He thought that this did not matter and we continued our conversation. Then, we came to the question of why I had come to Germany.

"I cannot understand at all," said the other guest, "what in the world do people whose grandpas and grandmas were German have to do with Germany. Such people have probably no personal connection to the country at all. On top of everything, they pretend to feel like Germans."

I was not given the chance to feel either really Bulgarian or really Israeli. Now, I was not given the chance to feel German either. Some guy, who could not tell a mosque from an Orthodox church, wanted to deny me

12 Franz Josef Strauss (1915-1988). German politician and Minister President of the state of Bavaria (1978-1988)

the right to have a connection to Germany and to feel that this country and this culture are close to me. Was I not cursed indeed?

The Little One was accepted as a third grader in a primary school in Munich. Frequently, kids wrote on the blackboard that he was stupid, because he did not speak German well enough. Sometimes, when he did not understand something, his teacher did not want to repeat it. She said always – he must learn to listen better. From anxiety and fear the boy started having hiccups and muscle cramps at night. They wanted to send him to a *school for foreigners*, since according to the teachers, "he had no chance to make the transition to a gymnasium (high school) in two years anyway."

. . .

Initially, after we moved to Munich from the North, my uncle, a cousin of my father's, invited us to stay with him and his wife. I had heard of him in Bulgaria, but my family was not in contact with him. I knew only that he was living in Munich. Soon after I arrived in Germany, I started calling everybody in Munich whose last name in the phone book was the same as mine. The thirteenth telephone number I dialed was his. After a long conversation over the phone, he invited us to visit. Later, he suggested that we should move to Munich and that we could stay with him for the time being. He thought that a big city such as Munich would offer many more job opportunities for me. I fell in love with this city the first time I set foot in it. My uncle was one of the nicest people I had ever known, and he was also the only living relative of my father's in Germany.

In the beginning of World War II, it was still possible for some Jews to pay their way out of a concentration camp. My uncle was in Auschwitz. A rich aunt from Vienna paid for him and bought his ship passage to China. At the time of Nazi Germany, Shanghai offered Jews the possibility to enter the country through their port without presenting any papers. Many Jews took this opportunity. This is how a large Jewish community was established in Shanghai. Then, in the early 1950s many of them emigrated to Israel or to America. After the war my uncle originally started working as a sailor on an Israeli ship. Later he moved back to Germany, the country that despite all that happened had remained the only real home for him.

We spent an unforgettable month with my uncle. Suddenly, however, he became ill and had to be hospitalized for a long time. His wife was just diagnosed with Alzheimer's. Because of my child, I could not stay alone with her at home. Thus, we had to find another solution, and we had to find it fast. I never intended to live in my uncle's place for long. Nevertheless, the plan was that I should find a job first, and then I could rent an apartment, something I had no chance to do while I was unemployed. For a period of time we had to sleep now with these friends, now with others. Sometimes it so happened that we would sleep in one place, eat in another, and take a shower in a third. Eventually, with the help of the social services, I got a room in an asylum home. It was unpleasant, even depressing. Nevertheless, we had peace at last. Soon after, I received a position at the University of Munich and could rent our own apartment. I also moved my son to a school in our neighborhood. This was a real piece of luck for him.

The boy came to the class of a teacher who became like a second father to him. This man and his entire family are among our most dear friends until today. My son's teacher showed an enormous amount of understanding and of patience. He asked me to meet him frequently and wanted to know everything about the boy. He wanted to help the child in every possible way and was always there for him. He called the attention of the rest of the children in the class to the fact that my son needed help and support. The kids started inviting my son to their homes and they were helping him with his homework. A few weeks after my son started going to the new school, he stopped having any hiccups and tics.

...

After he completed fourth grade the Little One went on to one of the best secondary schools in Munich, the humanistic Maximilian's Gymnasium. He was a good student, his classmates liked him, and he made friends who have been important in his life until today. Later, he won several awards for his academic work, earned his PhD at Cambridge University, and has built a career working in a number of international institutions. He can barely remember that once upon a time kids made fun of him in school.

"He will not be able to make the transition to secondary school anyway," said his first German teacher, who wanted to deny him the chance to try. The chance we owe to every single child in the world, for we have only borrowed our present from the future of our children.

Later, when my older son joined us, the wonderful teacher from the new school offered me his help again. I made virtually no decision with regard to the education of my children without consulting this man first. He talked to the Rector of the Maximilian's Gymnasium and my older son was accepted there as well. The Rector took him under his wing and was always inclined to resolve any kind of difficulties considering my son's interest.

"The most important thing is that the kid feels safe" he said once to me.

This school gave my children the support and the self-confidence they needed in order to adapt to a new and unknown world, and to find their way around in it. I am not sure to what degree they would have managed without the support of these two men.

...

Our family was reunited about five months after the Little One and I moved to Germany.

Years before I escaped my first husband had applied through a Bulgarian agency for a job abroad. This agency had the monopoly of sending specialists from different areas to developing countries supported by the former Soviet Union and generally by the Eastern Bloc. For many, this was the only possibility to make more money and to spend some time abroad. There were also others though who used those jobs as the only opportunity to escape from Bulgaria. If that was the case, people would spend some time in the respective developing country and they would put some money away. Then, on their way back to Bulgaria, they would disappear somewhere, perhaps first in one of the developing countries. We had in mind to do something similar. My husband signed a contract with the agency. He was supposed to teach political economy at the university level, either in Mozambique or in Angola. He was requested to take a six months language course in Portuguese at the Foreign Language Institute. His employer was under the obligation to give him a leave of absence for the entire duration of the course. The employment agency was paying him a salary and when he completed the course, he was able to return to his old job. However, in the next few years he was not sent to work abroad. We thought that we would never be able to leave the country and, with time, we gave up the developing countries idea. But shortly after the Little One and I had escaped, my husband was notified that he had to go to Angola. At that point, there was war in this country. There were no connections between Israel and Angola, not even telephone or postal services. My husband was supposed to teach in a military facility which was sealed off, and which no one could leave without a special permission. Our family would not have been able to be in any kind of contact at all. We discussed the situation, not directly, but through friends from Western Europe who were traveling on holidays to Bulgaria. My husband rejected the job. Then, the agency stuck his contract under his nose and insisted that he already had an obligation to them. In the meantime, my situation changed. I had moved to Germany. Had I applied for a family reunion, as we planned, we might have waited for many years before we could be reunited again. Thus, I came up with a different idea. I checked the routes of the airplanes to Angola. There were no direct flights from Sofia to Luanda. This meant that my husband and my son were going to have to make a stop either in Rome or in Lisbon. Maybe they could escape from the airport? This meant taking a great risk, but we decided to do it. So, my husband announced that he was ready to go to Angola. Now he was told that he could not take the boy along. It was terrible. My husband took the agency to court. He had to prove that he could not leave his child alone in Bulgaria. After long arguments he was allowed to travel with our son. The first one to get a passport was the child. His father did not know for a while whether he would receive a passport or not. The authorities were playing a cat-and-mouse game. In addition, my husband had to pay for the passports too, and the fees were very high. He sold everything valuable I had left behind – some gold coins from my father, and my piano. Every now and then he also gave some gifts, if he felt that this might help. Nothing helped. All of a sudden, my husband received his passport as well. This happened on Friday, before the Monday when the President of Germany, von Weizsäcker,[13] was to arrive on his first visit to Bulgaria. My husband and my son were told to leave Bulgaria on the Sunday before that. We will never know whether this was because the authorities were trying to avoid an international scandal, and whether there

[13] Richard Karl Freiherr von Weizsäcker (1920-2015). President of West Germany (1984-1990) and of the reunited Germany (1990-1994).

was a connection between my family's departure and von Weizsäcker's visit or not. In any event, I had threatened loud and clear, that "I would use my connections to the German government" and that I would "write about our family in the German press."

My son must have been very excited during the flight. My husband was aware of the fact that a Bulgarian airplane is considered Bulgarian territory. Anything could have happened to us if someone had managed to lure me into that plane using my son. Therefore, my husband had told our son to be very careful until they see me in Rome. He did not even allow the boy to eat the food in the plane because he was afraid that it might be poisoned or full of drugs. Such things were known to happen. In the plane with which my husband and my son flew to Rome, there was also a former colleague of mine. He started interrogating both father and son. Apparently, he wanted to know in the first place if they would see me in Rome. Perhaps this was one of the little games of the Bulgarian State Security.

During the three and a half hours while I was waiting outside at the airport in Rome, after the Bulgarian plane landed, I did not know whether I would have my son in my arms in the next few minutes, or whether he would be taken back to Bulgaria, or detained by the Italian authorities. I could barely survive this suspense and I just wanted all of this to be over.

I had friends who advised me about organizing this fleeing operation and I had friends who executed it. I have felt grateful to all of them every single day of my life. Out of respect for their privacy, I will not go into details here but I wish I could build a monument for them right here, at this very spot.

According to the plan design, I was supposed to wait outside, on the Italian side of the airport. I never went into the transit area. On the one hand, my friends were afraid that I could have a nervous breakdown. On the other hand, they did not want to give the Bulgarians any opportunity to blackmail me with my child. When I saw my son come through the glass door of border control I could not move at all. He approached me very slowly. I hugged him and did not let go of him until he said:

"Mamma, I cannot breathe."

In his own bed in Munich

First vacation, the Dolomites

Ablaze

When the Little One was in third grade his class was supposed to go on a one-week field trip to the countryside. Their teacher needed one more adult person to accompany them and I said I was available.

In my son's class there was a Turkish girl. Often, Muslim parents do not allow their daughters to stay anywhere overnight because of hygienic and religious reasons. However, the teacher thought it was very important that this girl should join her class on the trip. She had suffered some kind of a shock and all of a sudden had lost her speech without being disabled in any other way. Sometimes she would answer the teacher's questions briefly, but she refused to converse with anyone. The teacher was trying very hard to help her. He believed that the girl could relax from her anxiety and he thought that the atmosphere during the field trip could help her in that respect. He visited the parents and put a lot of effort into convincing them to let her go until they agreed.

During the field trip everything was going well. Even though the Turkish girl did not speak, she often seemed to be in high spirits and laughed very loud. One day, when the rest of the class went swimming with the teacher, I took her for a walk. I was talking to her as if she were answering. I told her about my son being laughed at in the old school, and how much courage and patience he needed to settle down in Germany. While I was talking to her, I felt that she took my hand. I kept talking. Suddenly she asked:

"Can I see you again after we get back to Munich?"

I pretended that nothing extraordinary had happened, but my heart was beating like mad. She was speaking again.

We got back to the country cottage for lunch. That day they served noodles with ham. The girl said nothing, but she did not touch the food because she did not eat pork. I went to the kitchen and asked the hostess, a hefty Bavarian woman, to give me a plate with noodles without the ham. She did not answer. She put some noodles on a plate, brought the plate to the dining room herself, dropped it on the table, pushed it roughly over to the girl, and said:

"If you Turks cannot get used to our rules, you should stay home or, better even, go back to where you belong."

The girl stopped talking again.

...

When the Berlin Wall fell I was overjoyed. I knew the Wall from the other side and I knew the Iron Curtain. The world seemed to start pursuing a new, wiser path. I sat for hours in front of the TV and could not believe that such a miracle had happened. I was happy to be able to experience those times.

I had a very good friend in Berlin whom I had known since my childhood in Bulgaria. Under communism he had had problems with the Stasi[14] and he even spent some time in prison. Later, he started coming often to Bulgaria for professional reasons but there he also met a woman from West Berlin. He was over fifty when he married her. However, he was never allowed to go to West Berlin. If I remember correctly, the East German authorities allowed his wife to visit him only a few times in East Berlin, and only very briefly. After a few years they had a child, who lived with the mother in the Western part of the city. The family was not allowed to be united. Neither could the father go to his son nor the son to his father. The only place in the world where all three of them could be together was Bulgaria. For years the mother and the child were coming on vacation to Bulgaria from the West, and the father from the East, in order to spend a little time together. On the morning after the Berlin Wall had fallen, my friend called.

"Do you know what I am doing right now?" he asked. "I am making breakfast for my son. I am with him in his home for the very first time."

...

I was particularly interested to learn about the changes in Bulgaria. I was listening to the BBC and Radio Free Europe, and I was really excited to hear about the founding of the first democratic organization, the *Club for the Defense of Glasnost and Perestroika.* When the names of the founders were mentioned in a broadcast, I realized that these were people who, for

[14] German. Ministerium für Staatssicherheit (Ministry for State Security). The secret police agency of GDR (East Germany).

a very long time, had been trying to prepare in different ways for political changes.

After the fall of Zhivkov I called many of my Bulgarian friends around the world. We congratulated each other and we celebrated. Before I escaped from Bulgaria, I could not imagine that one day there could be any demonstrations or students' strikes in Sofia, and now I was sorry I was not part of them.

Soon, one of my best friends, Philip Dimitrov, was elected Chair-person of the Union of Democratic Forces. He visited me in Munich. We couldn't stop talking. He needed people he could rely on. I could not and I did not want to return, nevertheless, I wanted to help. There were things one could do from abroad. We organized aid transports with medications, clothes, and food. We gave talks to explain the socio-political situation at the time. We also tried to support the first democratic election campaign by sending money, copy machines, fax- machines and other materials.

Quite soon, however, people whom I knew from the old communist milieu started appearing in Germany and asserting their "democratic" views and their membership in the newly founded parties. Acquaintances, who used to be communists or who had desired to be accepted in the communist party, were now fighting on the side of the democratic movement and denying their past. Something similar must have been happening in all countries of the former Eastern Bloc.

The elections of 1991, when Philip Dimitrov became prime minister, brought big hopes. This would be the wrong place to discuss why he later failed as head of the government. There are different opinions in that regard, and at the time I was too far away from everything that was happening in Bulgaria. Here, I would only like to tell a story about something that touched me deeply as a human being and a friend.

The heads of the leaders in the young democratic movement in Bulgaria were falling one after the other. Major personalities turned out to be in fact, or at least allegedly, opportunists or collaborators in the State Security. The honesty of most of them was brought into disrepute. Nevertheless, numerous attempts to discredit the new prime minister failed. Dimitrov's past was so clean and his morality as a truly religious person were so convincing that any attempt to slander him was in vain. As a young man Dimitrov was interested in psychology and philosophy. His excellent foreign language skills allowed him to read, in the original, works which other Bulgarians had no access to. Philip Dimitrov was a follower of the first real Freudian in Bulgaria after the war, Dr. Georgi Kamenov. In the 1970s, Dimitrov became the head of the new *help-group for psychoanalysis and psychotherapy,* established at the *Academy of Medicine*, which he led in cooperation with psychologists and psychiatrists. At a certain point, Dimitrov stepped back as a leader of this group and dedicated his entire time to his profession as a lawyer. In 1992 the propaganda tried to invent some kind of a mental disease on the basis of Dimitrov's interest in the Freudian movement in Bulgaria. Nobody was able to say anything concrete about it. As was very common in Bulgaria before the changes, now too the propaganda was operating with quasi-information and with quasi-truth. Dimitrov's opponents were saying simply that once upon a time he had something to do with psychiatry, and "thus, he must have a screw loose himself." Many of Dimitrov's colleagues, with whom he had worked in the psychotherapy group, reacted immediately and clarified the simple facts. Nevertheless, all who knew Philip Dimitrov were left with a bad taste in the mouth. I thought of the evenings when he was reading to me from the books he had written; of his dreams which never implied greed for power; of the fact that unlike many of his friends, he believed in the peaceful and sensible political development of Bulgaria that could unfold without bloodshed and witch-hunts; and I thought of the personal sacrifices he had to make after the changes in order to make himself available to the democratic movement. I thought also of the excellent speeches he gave in the U.S.A. and of the vote of confidence in 1992 when the communists insisted that Dimitrov would damage the international reputation of Bulgaria. I thought that throughout history, one way or another, through one party or another, Bulgaria has always destroyed or betrayed its best people.

...

At the time I had already for a few years had a second job as interpreter for the *Bundesamt for the Recognition of Foreign Refugees.* The officials I met were good people who showed a lot of patience and understanding for the extremely diverse categories of refugees they had to deal with. Frequently, they had to listen to made-up stories or even to tolerate threats; they had to welcome small children in a friendly way, and they had to calm down mothers. Day after day these people had to tell truth and deception apart.

A very well organized and profitable refugee-business was established in the former Eastern Bloc. Truck drivers competed in offering to smuggle people through the borders illegally. Adventurous entrepreneurs organized bus trips for illegal immigrants and advertised non-existent dream-jobs in provincial towns and villages. Pimps trafficked girls who looked exotic and who, in their hope for a better life, vanished somewhere among the drug addicts and the wealthy marriage imposters. Some states were offered millions if they took their refugees back from Germany. From 1991/92 on, people could purchase their "freedom" from international smugglers for 250 Deutsche Marks. Applications for political asylum were submitted by the same person in different Bundesländer (federal states) in Germany, or even in different countries. People collected welfare, went back to their home country for a short while, and then came again to the West to collect more and more welfare.

Regardless, there was another side of the coin too but there was a tendency to turn a blind eye to that other side, so that one did not have to look for excuses for the fact that the *Iron Curtain* that had fallen only recently, was now being rebuilt in the West.

At an internal conference in London in the autumn of 1993 the BBC showed a film about Bulgarian asylum seekers who were rejected by the Swedish government and deported back to Bulgaria. Children, who had been educated in Sweden and who, meanwhile, had almost forgotten how to speak Bulgarian, were speaking to Swedish journalists in perfect Swedish. They were talking about their friends and classmates, about their neighbors and their teachers, about the letters they kept receiving from Sweden. In fact, they were talking about a country they had become used to and where they felt at home; about a world that, with their return to Bulgaria, had collapsed and was hopelessly lost forever. These were the confused souls of children who would never know where they came from and where they belonged – children who were doomed to lose the best they could have ever had when they were only eight or nine – the sense of comfort and safety. Two fathers who were in Sweden with their families committed suicide, hoping that Sweden would allow their families to stay. One of them was thirty, the other one thirty-five; one was an engineer, the other an auto mechanic. Both of them had no political reasons for asylum, according to the law.

"They should not be sent to small communities. They should not be allowed to build their nests," an official from the Bundesamt who had the authority to make such decisions said once to me. "Once they are known in the community and everything gets to a more personal level, it would be much more difficult to get rid of them."

Consequently, we needed an impersonal world, and we were about to build it.

...

For most officials the situation with the war refugees from the former Yugoslavia was clear without any doubt. Shadow-humans whose past was bombed to pieces or burnt to the ground, and whose future was supposed to be erected from the ashes.

When war refugees from the Balkans started coming to Germany I was working in the Bundesamt almost every day. Together with the decision-makers, as the officials in this office were called. We shared the pain and the sorrow, and we laughed about the fabricated stories we got to listen to every now and then. A particularly human atmosphere predominated in this office, for we all were much exposed to the horrors of life. One day, I wanted to have a cup of coffee in the common room, as usual. Another colleague, a German, was there too. I took the only clean coffee cup available and I was going to pour some coffee in it.

"Careful!" screamed my colleague. "This is not the first time you are doing this. Each one of us here has his/her own cup, with a particular color. Only the white cups are for the interpreters. Otherwise we will mix our saliva, and God knows how well the cups are washed."

I easily get disgusted. I do not allow even my children to drink from my cup, unless I am sure it is well washed. I would have been the first one to appreciate an initiative for everyone, but really everyone, in the office to have their own cup. However, I found it remarkable that interpreters could mix their saliva among themselves, but not with German saliva.

...

Hoyerswerda[15] was a shock to all. I could never imagine that living in Germany today I would fall asleep with the memory of such tragedy or that I would wake up fearing this could happen again. However, it seemed that we people are pretty strange in our daily life, when things take their normal course.

When I immigrated to Germany the predominant atmosphere in governmental and administrative offices was very different from that in the beginning of the 1990s. When I was new in the country I felt that regardless of how unkind officials might be they were aware of the fact that a foreigner was to a degree protected by the law. Officials did not allow themselves to express certain thoughts and feelings they had. Rather, they were trying to suppress them. However, by the beginning of the 1990s I witnessed how the political commotions caused many people to change deep inside, in step with the common xenophobic delirium – consciously or unconsciously. In fact, people changed much quicker than the laws.

Television offered then all possible information. Live. Directly in one's living room. The burning asylum home; the Turkish women killed in Mölln and Solingen; the German "soldiers" fighting as volunteers on the side of the Chetniks in the former Yugoslavia, who, extending their right arms, yelled "heil" in front of the camera; the mutilated war victims; the raped women from Sarajevo and Bihać; the innocent little children, picked up by the humanitarian aid convoys. Representatives of different political parties were invited to a public event, in order to answer questions about the current socio-political developments. Schwabing, one of the fanciest neighborhoods in Munich, announced "An Evening with Enzensberger."[16] The program included a reading from his latest book *The Great Migration*. After that there was a discussion with party representatives on the agenda. The discussion began. We heard some restless voices, a lot of nonsense, and some sensible comments. At some point the word was given to the representative of the SPD (Social Democratic Party of Germany). According to her, we had to admit that "we all feared the foreign."

---

15 German town in the state of Saxony, former East Germany. In September 1991, after several days of xenophobic riots, petrol bombs were thrown at a hostel for asylum seekers.

16 Hans Magnus Enzensberger, born 1929. German author, poet, translator, and editor.

Question from the audience:

"What do you mean by fearing the foreign?"

SPD representative:

"It is obvious, isn't it? Imagine you are in the metro. Suddenly a colored man gets in. The first thing that we all feel is fear, a simple shock."

I do not like getting involved in public discussions. Nevertheless, I cried out spontaneously:

"This is your own problem. Why do you say 'we all'?"

Voices from the audience:

"Well, in fact that is true. We should be honest, shouldn't we?"

The discussion turned into an unbelievable presentation of statistics showing how many percent of the German female population, according to some survey, could imagine having sex with a colored man, and how many thought this impossible. I left the event.

...

Once I had to go again to a small town to interpret for asylum applicants. The shelter for the refugees and the immigration offices were in the same building. Exhausted human figures were drifting in the lower floors, dragging some pillows and blankets. The staircase stank like sweat and dirty laundry. Underwear, socks, and shirts were hanging from the windows to dry. There wasn't enough space – either for the people or for their luggage. Old and young were sitting on the floors of the corridors, waiting to be registered for interviews in the upper floors of this *Titanic*. Mothers were breastfeeding their babies amongst the crowd, children were crying with hunger – quietly and patiently.

The elevator served only the upper floor. The rooms there were locked. Despite that, every now and then Africans, Arabs, Chinese and Romanians, Bulgarians, Croats, and Serbs, managed to get upstairs. By contrast, none of the staff had ever set foot in the living quarters downstairs.

Suddenly, around noon there was panic in the building. Everybody was running around. Doors were being opened and shut. There had been a bomb threat. The building had to be cleared. All the people inside were evacuated.

For a while, we stood downstairs on the street, at some distance from the building, waiting to hear the explosion. Scared and silent, we did not move from the spot and we kept looking at the house.

There was no explosion. Most likely, it was false alarm. Specialists searched the building and two hours later we were allowed to go back in.

We calmed down. The day took its usual course. People were registered and interviewed. Paperwork was sorted out, and children were breastfed in the corridors again. Around four o'clock most officials left. I had to sort out something else, and then I left too. I walked slowly away from the building. It was sunny and green. It had rained and I could see big drops of rain still hanging in the grass, like bewildered eyes. They were glittering and smiling and wishing one "a nice evening." I did not take the metro. I wanted to walk. It was shopping time, since, at the time, stores had to close at six. A smell of fresh wholegrain bread and rolls came out of the small, pretty bakeries. When I got to Munich, I walked through the Viktualienmarkt and got cheese and honey from the barrow across from the church tower of St. Peter. I would go soon again to the tower with the Little One. He loved the city. He knew every single detail about the history of the establishment of Munich, and he loved showing guests the old city. He went up the tower as often as he could to see the city from above. I had to go by way of Marienplatz. It was around five. There was no Glockenspiel at this time of the day. I took my time. The new Rathaus soared to the sky in its soft white robe and looked at me gently through its many window-eyes. In the very beginning, when I did not know anyone in Munich but my uncle, I made friends with this wonderful monument. All windows and doors were then closed to us and we could see them only from the outside. In those days my son and I went often to Marienplatz. The Rathaus always reminded us that, in fact, we were very fortunate to be living in this city. Our doctor and our dentist were also at Marienplatz – the first doors that were opened for us. I continued walking up the Theatinerstraße, and past Odeonsplatz and the Feldherrnhalle. Under the Nazis, Hitler's bust was placed here and every man who passed by had to bow down or take off his hat. I learned this from Alfred Andersch. I had translated his short stories into Bulgarian when I was still living in Sofia. His stories play frequently in Munich. In order to imagine the details of his descriptions I had to learn a lot about the city. The first time I came to Munich from Northern Germany, I already knew what color the water in the lake in the English Garden was going to be, how high the Chinese tower was, and which streets one had to take to avoid walking by the Feldherrnhalle. Meanwhile Munich had become my home and I loved it. I liked it even when the weather was bad and also in every season of the year. I could stroll through the city for hours and I never got tired or bored. But now it was time to start moving faster. My children must have come home a while ago. They must have done their homework and were probably hungry. Later, I had to go to a parent conference. There had been no other time in my life when I was as happy with my work as the time at Ludwig-Maximilian-University. I was given every possible opportunity to develop further professionally and to be completely fulfilled. I was also free to teach and to publish what I thought appropriate. I was able to read, write, study, listen to, and look at whatever I wished. I could go regularly to a philosophical school for comparative study of religion, without having to feel like a criminal. I could talk to my children about my views, without being afraid that by doing this I might hinder their adjustment to society. Most importantly, my children were able to dream. Regardless of the problems this society had, it was a free society. It was up to the person to choose what to represent in that society.

For a short time it rained again and then it stopped. I took a deep breath of the fresh Munich air and I thought that if I had to take the same long path again, because all of this was somewhere far away, I would not hesitate to do it.

Papa

My Parents

My boys

Two Happy Brothers

J.'s Wedding in the Philippines – with his wife, his mother, and both his fathers.

A Picnic in Central Park, New York

Peter's 50th Reunion in Oxford

With Papa

New York

Forgiveness. Mosaic Mural by Calin Trenkov-Wermuth

Albergo del Sole. Prologue to Part II

In the center of Rome, the Pantheon – a temple dedicated to every god – has been standing, untouched by time or nature, for over two thousand years. Commissioned originally by the statesman Marcus Agrippa, son-in-law of Augustus, and arguably rebuilt by Hadrian, it has buried the name of its ingenious architect in the light of sun and moon coming through the open dome, as if focusing the love of the gods on the unlimited capacity of the human mind. Was Apollodorus of Damascus the man who caught the feelings of the gods in the oculus of this dome? Perhaps. We cannot be certain. But we know this – it was a human being – one from that distant ancient world that taught us so much about mathematics, about astronomy, about architecture, and about art, philosophy, and politics.

In the 7th century CE, the Christians took over the Pantheon and started using it as a church, known today as *Santa Maria della Rotonda.* A few centuries earlier, in 336 they had also taken over the date of the winter solstice festival which was celebrated as the date of the rebirth of the sun god in one of the last official religions of the late Roman empire, Solus Invictus. At the time of the first Christian Roman emperor, Constantine the Great, Christians started celebrating the birth of Jesus on the same date and a few years later December 25th was officially declared as the birth of Jesus by Pope Julius I.

Different forms of worship of the sun were indigenous to the Romans and have evidently existed since the kingdom of the Sabines, long before the founding of Rome. Solus Invictus, the invincible sun god, represented a particular aspect of the sun – its all-giving power and strength. The cult was still popular at the time of Saint Augustine. Throughout history, temples have often been transformed, especially churches into mosques and mosques into churches. Think about Hagia Sophia for example. Today, Santa Maria della Rotonda functions as a Roman Catholic Church but it is located in the Roman Pantheon. People go to Piazza al Pantheon, they look at the Roman temple, they learn that this is the best-preserved ancient building in Europe, and they remember it as . . . the Pantheon. There is some enormous mystical power which has taken hold of this temple. It is protective and rejuvenating, inspiring and dominating. Nothing has destroyed that power, as nothing has destroyed the temple itself. It cannot be the power of history, of time, or of civilization. We have destroyed so many of their creations. Could it be the power of all gods being celebrated together?

In one of the corners of the piazza, to the left of the Pantheon when you look at the portico, there is an old hotel (*albergo*) documented since 1467 as *Sole al Pantheon*. Its symbol, attached to the outside wall in the form of a beautiful copper gravure, is a large image of the sun, with its rays looking like a lion's mane around the serious face of an old wise being, the sun itself, watching over the Pantheon. On the gravure, there is also a sheep. No one could tell me what that symbol meant or what its origins were. There is nothing about its history in the brochure of the hotel or on the web. Was the owner who built this inn in the 15th century pagan? Did he worship the sun god? Was he fascinated with the temple of all gods? Did he want to honor the sun as well the Christian symbol of the Lamb of God? I will never know.

I did not know that I had stayed in this hotel on that memorable night when my son and I fled communism many years ago. Until my son remembered this and told me.

I wrote the first part of my memoir only a few years after we escaped. Now, looking at the hotel Albergo del Sole twenty-five years later, the memories of that time were still fresh and vivid in my head. I could recall the wretched fights for some freedom of spirit that I had dedicated my life to; I could see the events of each day during our escape in front of my eyes; I could hear my own thoughts, still beating in my head like the pulse of a scared heart; I could hear the unusually wise and calming words of my little son who never lost his peace of mind, and who grew up mentally with every hour, for he was trying to help the mother he loved. But I could not remember the names of all the places we had stopped at in fear. Would we be recognized? Would we be sent away? Would we find food? Would we have to hide?

When I was little ancient myths were often my bedside stories. The history of Rome was a dinner table subject my mother never ceased to discuss. The images of the Pantheon and the Colosseum from her albums with photographs of Roman architectural monuments were as familiar to me as the local church around the corner. But after my son and I spent our first night in the free world, in Rome, I could never draw a map of that city in my head in order to return to the old hotel in which we stayed back then. I did not remember even the fact that the piazza in front of that hotel was the one at the Pantheon. But my son did. He returned to Rome for the first time eighteen years later. He walked around the city and he remembered. He drew that imaginary map of our night in Rome, he followed those vague memories of a time he will never forget, he reached the Piazza al Pantheon, he looked at the temple of all gods, and he knew he had been there. He looked around the piazza, he looked at each corner, and there it was – our hotel. He walked in and recognized the stairs and the lobby. He was back in that unforgettable night. He bought a card with a photograph of the old hotel and mailed it to me. "This is where we were," he wrote. "The name of our hotel is Albergo del Sole – Shelter of the Sun." Ever since he sent me that postcard, we wanted to go back to Rome together. We did. We went to Rome to celebrate the 25th anniversary of our freedom.

We visited Rome for a few days, but we spent only the last night in "our" hotel. In the evening, he and I sat at the piazza for hours, looking at the Pantheon. Things were different now. My life went in front of me as on a film tape. I was the one who stood here a quarter of a century ago – a woman with her eight year old child; a woman who had to leave her other son behind as a pawn to a totalitarian regime that needed to make sure all citizens who were allowed to travel abroad (even if not to the West) would return; a woman who did not know where she and her child would sleep, where they would live, and what they would eat; a woman whose previous life had died, except for her child left behind; a woman who was beginning a new life. I had taken enormous responsibility for the child who was with me and for the one who was not.

But now, twenty-five years later, I was also someone who was a tourist in Rome. I wanted to see the sights of a city I was teaching about in my ancient literature classes. So, while on vacation I spent first a week in Sorrento, together with my husband, and then I came to Rome to meet my son – the one with whom I escaped. Could I relate to my old self? Was this life today more my life than that of the first night in Rome twenty-five years ago? Did I have a life back then at all? Or did I have just my kids whose life

I wanted to build? Was I still the German Jew coming from Bulgaria or was I the American coming from New York? Could one of my lives have erased the other? How many lives did I have? How many lives did my sons have? What made up the fiber of my identity, or of the identity of my children?

Some people tell me my sons are real world-citizens. Others ask me where I feel at home, whether I knew where I belonged, or if I had any sense of identity at all. The truth is I have never had any identity crisis. Nor did my children. I have never felt that I was not at home anywhere in the world, except in the country where I was born and where I had no freedom. I do not believe that we have to have roots in only one country, in only one culture or in only one religion. I believe that our roots are in being human and in living with a beautiful and generous being which we keep abusing and misusing because we do not understand that this is where our roots are – our incredibly patient planet. Nevertheless, because of all these questions people always ask me, I have been wondering what makes up our identity.

It is my conviction that identity has its own life and that the type of a process in which individual identity is formed must be different in each particular case. The kind of material that makes up one's identity seems to vary from person to person. I also believe that, if we are aware of the way we live, then we can choose, and we can form our identity ourselves. So, I want to explore what makes up my own identity and, perhaps, the identity of the people close to me. Is it what we do or what we think, or feel? Is identity rooted in the place we live in or in the language we speak? A simple answer would be that all of this applies. This may well be true but there must be a mechanism that keeps a certain identity alive. For some identities appear to die, I think. One thought I have always had about my own identity was that it was based on dreams. I do not mean this in Freudian terms. What I mean is the process of powerful wishing, hoping, and willing that the human being is capable of.

That night, on the first of July 2012, when my son and I were sitting in one of the corners of Piazza al Pantheon, I fell into a very sentimental mood and I told him that I missed the time of the early days after the escape – when we were dreaming, when everything was ahead of us, when our life expected us to start living it.

Albergo del Sole. Prologue to Part II

25 Years Later

"Remember our walk on the *Tayelet*, the promenade in Tel Aviv? Remember how we were looking at the sunset and we were dreaming of where we want to live and what we want our life to be like?" I said nostalgically. "Wasn't that the most beautiful time of our life? I wish I could go back to that time."

"Nonsense," my son said to my surprise. "Do you remember what we were dreaming of? To have a home, to find work for you so that we can buy food, to find a good school for me, so that I have a good education and I could learn what I wanted to learn, without anyone telling me what I may or may not read – as they did with you in Bulgaria. And for you? To be able to write – without being told what to write and what not to write about. We wanted to be able to study – so many things, we wanted to be able to help other people. Most of all, we wanted my brother and my father to be free too, and we wanted to see them again. Now we have all of this . . . , and you want to go back to the time when we didn't?"

My son spoke wisely then. We did have all we used to dream of. And we did not want to change any bit of our life, for all of it, together, was the path that led us to today.

Part II

A MIGRANT'S MANDALA

To my Sons

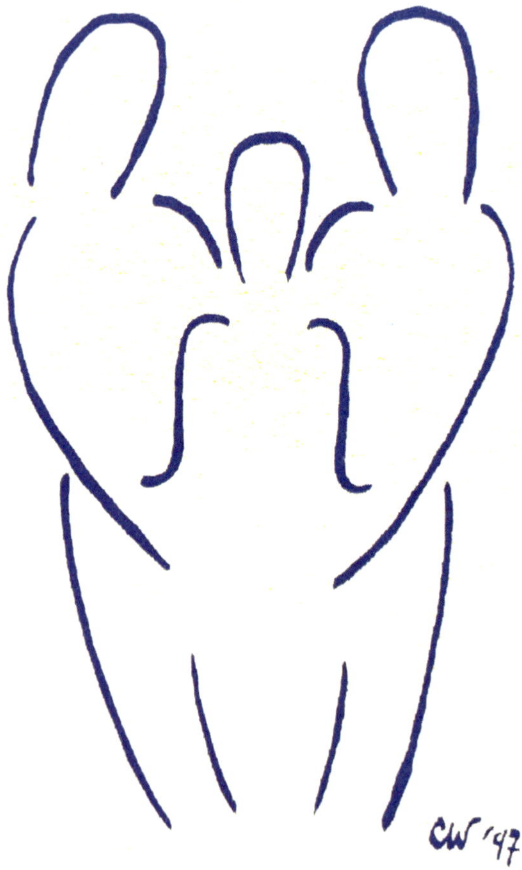
CW '97

A Tablet of Stone

"He who saw the Deep... He came a far road, was weary, found peace, and set all his labors on a tablet of stone."[17]

It was the touch of cool salt water, the closeness of the distance I felt while looking at the silver-blue horizon of the open sea, that first took me far from the reality around me when I was little and that, like a gift of all gods and of all times, placed on the wet palm of my hand the belief that I could reach a dream. Every time I smelled salt in the air, every time I thought of the oneness of all water on earth, I knew that someday I would get beyond the end of the horizon. I was little then, and I did not know the horizon had no end. I thought of myself as a small particle of this universe of waves and with the waves, I thought, I could leave one place, one plane, one life, and go far away – to another. It was all a matter of thinking, I believed, and the sea, with its long, thick, dark-blue eyelashes, winked at me in confirmation; free I will be, I thought; free to go to the other end of the water. I never learned how to sail, but how to be free I did learn.

...

Writing the second part of my memoir, more than thirty years after I wrote the first, is to me like making a mandala; it is a meditation on the composition of a human life – my life. Years ago, I met two Buddhist monks in the Phuktal Gompa, a monastery near the town of Khangsar in the Indian part of the Tibetan plateau. The two men had been working on their clay mandala for more than ten years. They never stopped, except to sleep, eat, and pray. While working on the clay with their fingers, as if they played the harp, the monks kept chanting. In the ancient texts of the Rig Veda, the concept *mandala* is related to the notion of a container where sacred mantras or hymns are collected. The sounds of those mantras were believed to have manifested in different forms in the creation of the world. The two monks of Phuktal Gompa were chanting and working on

[17] *The Epic of Gilgamesh*. Penguin Books, 1999. I:1-10

their mandala in order to maintain the process of constant re-creation of the world. This is why the symbol of the mandala is a symbol of the universe. This part of the book then, shall be my chanting in the process of the constant recreation of the world – at least of my world. It shall be a book of concepts and impressions, the clay pieces of my mandala – the pieces of life, the substance of re-creating myself.

What are the things that are formative to us? How do we think of them and how do we remember them? How do we experience them – the sensations, feelings, impressions, the logical constructs in memory? What are the associations we make between different things and why do we make them? When we think of something, when we believe or when we draw a conclusion, or make a decision – how much is that based on associations that pop-up in our memory – a question discussed so much in theory? How are the experiences we had represented in our memory? Or in a book? How do we represent? How am I the person I am? Descartes, Montaigne, and many others have stressed the importance of thinking. I am wondering if we could say: look at the things I think of, and you would know who I am.

A book, of course, (and any other text) cannot be a mirror image of the processes in my head. It is a created construct, a *poesis*. But it comes as close as possible to the real process which may or may not be controllable. So, let us say – my book is a controlled representation of my thinking. Is this stream of consciousness? Perhaps. Or even a stream of both consciousness and the unconscious. However, my point here is not to further develop the literary stream-of-consciousness method. I am interested in the essential material that makes up an individual's world, and that, I believe, begins with the making-up of our own thoughts, feelings, impressions; with the composing of concepts, beliefs, and character – in other words it begins with composing ourselves. Doesn't life remind you of a mandala? And don't we create the world by constantly re-creating ourselves?

History, as twisted and manipulated as it has always been, is memory of sorts. I think every writer should pay attention to a bit of history in their work. After all, without memory we could not create even two lines of literature. What happens to Alzheimer's patients can easily happen to civilization if the connections of history, the connections between different times, cultures, works of art, philosophical schools, law and religious systems are irreparably destroyed and forgotten. The memory of our world or of history is the functioning brain of civilization. It is our *Manda-la*, or essence in a container. Literature is history too, and so are art, and music, and architecture – the clay tablets that humans have engraved on their intellectual development. Here, then, is my mandala – a memoir, a collection of impressions, feelings, memories – all clay pieces in the history of our world.

Making a Mandala

The Home Valley

Today, I often look at myself as if from above, as if I am alien and new to me. I see *me*, and I am wondering what I am doing, where I am. A Monarch butterfly spends a whole life traveling, guided by some incomprehensible forces, until it rests under the moist crowns of the trees in Michoacán, without ever going back where it came from. I seem to be no more than a migrant creature that, like a Monarch butterfly, has reached its destination and does not wish to journey anywhere again.

Often, I have been asked where I was from, where was home. I never liked that question. In fact, I have many homes. They all mean a lot to me. However, I certainly did not feel that I had a home in all the places where I have lived. I believe that I have figured what made some places home to me, and when did I not feel at home. And no, I have never forgotten the beginning of my journey – not ever.

. . .

Around five in the evening, when the day realized that it was time to go and the night impatiently waited to take its place, when the sky was crimson, and the chimneys started scribbling the histories of homes into the air, the cows were coming down the hills – slowly, lazy, thirsty, and tired from the sticky summer heat. They toddled downhill from all sides toward the village that was curled up in the valley between the gradually rising mountain peaks. The sound of cow bells came down with the sun, as if it too would set – a steady orchestration, as harmony to the church bell of the monastery nearby. Ding, ding – dong, dong, dang, dang, diiiiiing . . . . Chang, chang, chang! Each one sounded differently, for they had to be recognized. Once the cows had reached the village, the cowherd would let them find their way home by themselves. They stopped here and there, usually at the troughs – to gulp some water after the long day in the dryness of the hills; they looked at one another, and then they continued walking – with the certainty of nature, each to the gate of their own home. The farmers waited for them outside. They had to open and to close the gates, and to go have supper, comforted that their cows were nicely fed and that they were back. Often, one could see neighbors standing at the gates and talking to each other: "Belka must be lost again, I hear her too far on the left." "Well, and Sivushka is behind again. She must be getting old."

Each household had a cow or two and there was only one way to know when the cows were coming back – by the sound of their bells. There was about one hour in each day, except on Sundays, when one could listen to the music of the cow-bells – the *chans*. Their distinct voices sounded as if someone has orchestrated a melody. Indeed, there is a region in Bulgaria in the Rhodope mountains, where in olden times the *chan* was treated as a musical instrument. People there used to call the early evening a time when the chans sing. Unless some cow was lost, the valley would eventually stop singing. That was supper time in the village. The bells were silent, the lights behind the windows were on, the water in the river was getting darker and darker with every minute, the sky had the color of the mud in front of the small huts, the chimney smoke was ghostly, and there was no one in the open any longer.

All this I saw in Bistritsa, a small village near Sofia, in the heart of the mountain Vitosha. The village was named after one of the two streams that ran through it. The name means clear water. Our family owned a piece of land there on which in the 1960s my parents built a summer house. Back then this was a distant village, about an hour and a half away from the city.

The first time I got off the bus in the middle of the village square, the *megdan*, aged eight, I was struck by the smell. The cool fresh mountain air was mixed with the strong scent of grass, wildflowers, and cow dung. Near the bus stop, there was a bread bakery where twice a day one could buy fresh bread, just taken out of the oven. It was as if its smell covered me like a blanket – warm and soft. The *megdan* was paved with large cobble stones. It had not changed for ages, since the time when Bulgaria was still part of the Ottoman Empire. Across from the bus stop was the village inn, the *khan*. In front of the *khan*, there was a big loud crowd. It was Sunday. Sunday used to be the day for weddings in Bulgaria. My mother explained that the crowd we were looking at was a wedding procession. It must have started from the home of the groom, whose family were going to pick up the bride.

When we got off the bus, the wedding procession was proceeding to the townhall to witness the civil marriage, which was supposed to be performed by a townhall clerk. After the short official ceremony, the party gathered on the *megdan* to dance in a *khoro* – a circle dance. It was beautiful to look at it. The folk costumes which in my early childhood people in the countryside were still wearing on holidays, were very colorful, with handmade embroidery of various elaborate patterns. The combination of long snow-white laced undershirt with the bright red, blue, green and yellow of the sleeveless top dress for women, the *sukman*, and the men's trousers, *poturi,* and vest, *elek,* appeared as shiny and as fresh as the wildflowers on the meadows of this mountain village.

The most fascinating thing about the Bulgarian *khoro* is the distinct and complicated steps. Different from other circle dances that I have seen later in my life around the world, the art of the *khoro* is not only in creating different shapes with the line of people, but also in the technique of the complex and varied steps. The music for the *khoro* came from across the street where two men were playing folk instruments. I was still looking around, overwhelmed by the smell of dung and fresh bread, when I heard the long sad sound of a *gaida*, a bagpipe typical in the Balkan countries, especially in mountain regions. The *gaida* began to sound a little more playful and jolly until it was joined by the *kaval*, a wooden wind instrument similar to the panpipe. Gradually, a thin supple line of people separated from the big group gathered in front of the *khan* and spread out around the whole *megdan* in light dancing steps. A big tall man was leading the *khoro*, his left hand on his hip, waiving a white lace handkerchief with his right hand.

We had to leave the *megdan* before the wedding celebration was over. We took the steep street uphill, straight toward the mountain. We followed the stream on the left. Then we crossed it, in order to take a parallel path between the two streams, to get to our piece of land. That land was large, empty, and covered with old wild sycamores. In the middle, it was divided by a tiny little brook whispering quietly and gently. Back then, there weren't many houses around us – only a new village house on the lower side, and a nice old villa in a rustic style at the back.

Before we built the house, my parents used to rent a room in the village, so that we could spend more time there. I loved the contrast to the city life. The smells, the quiet, the fresh bread, the nettle fields, and the hazelnut bushes. Our breakfast milk came from the neighbor's cow, the eggs were collected every morning in the coop in our hosts' yard, and I could play along the streams and run up the hills all day long with other children from the village, until I was exhausted and had to go back home, together with the cows.

My favorite season in Bistritsa was the fall. After the harvest people used to gather in groups in the evening to peel the corn, to clean the beans and the hazelnuts, and to string the red pepper for drying. While they were working, they sang folk songs, they told tales, and they joked with one another. I wish I could say that this was how I spent my whole childhood, but it wasn't. Those memories belong only to the first few years in Bistritsa. They remained in my heart forever, and they made me love telling stories. But things changed rapidly. By the time I was twelve, there was no cobbled pavement in the village, the road between the two streams was covered with asphalt, the young people replaced the folk dress with cheap mini-skirts and jeans, and, on holidays only the elderly kept dancing *khoro* in the center of the village, which everyone started calling a *square*.

I spent a lot of time in Bistritsa: every summer, all holidays, and almost every weekend. It was the place I loved most when I was still in Bulgaria, and it was the place I missed most after I left.

In the year I turned sixty, my mother died. I was no one's child any longer – both my parents, who had built the house, were gone.

"You have no feelings for the house," said my sister. "You have distanced yourself from it. To you, it is not a home, it is just property," she proclaimed.

She thought she knew.

We sold my part of the land and the house which my sister and I shared. There was no longer a home for me to return to in Bulgaria.

The truth is that I did not miss much after I escaped. My life under the communist regime had been so restricted, so uncertain, so full of fear, that it made the country I was born in feel less like my home than many other places I lived in later. The things I loved in Bulgaria, that also left a deep mark in my life, were Bistritsa, the amazing mountains, the Black Sea, and some people. They have always been in my mind and in my feelings, but they felt closer to me after I left than while I was living in the country of my birth.

. . .

Bulgaria is a country that many could not place on the map. Sometimes, when I say where I was born, people ask me if the capital is Bucharest. *Wrong country,* I think, *but… never mind*! Every now and then I tried to skip these uncomfortable conversations by saying that I was from Germany, since I am half German indeed. Germany, however, reminded people of the war and of the Nazis, so that often I had to specify that my father was a German Jew. On occasion, that explanation did not make me popular either and with time I realized that, in my case, there was no satisfactory answer to the question: "Where are you from?" I have never been sure what people wanted me to say. Where am I from? When I say I am from New York, people ask: "yeah, but where is home?" Home, in fact, is in midtown Manhattan. It is an old apartment from the 1930s, where I cook dinner for my husband and my sons. It is where I have my desk to read and write, to grade my students' papers, where I take a shower and get dressed to go to work in the morning, and where, in the evening, I go to bed, exhausted, without having ever finished everything I needed to do. Home is where my husband came back to, after they put two stents in his main artery, and where I brought him after he survived his cancer surgery. Home is where my sons are for the holidays. Home is where I found my family, safe and sound, after having walked for an hour and a half from my office on September 11th, without being able to reach any one of my three men by phone, without knowing if at the end of that walk I would find all of them, or two of them, or one, or none. It is the place I go back to – from wherever I have been – that is my home today. "But, obviously, you haven't started here," they say. I have not! But I have started several times in several different places, and I have had several homes in my life. Does this make me homeless? No! It makes me rich.

"But have you never felt that you lack identity?"

"Never!"

"But where do you belong?"

To what I love. That makes me who I am. And only after that, the places that have been home to me, including those which are only in my memory today.

I grew up with the smell of my father's pipe, my mother's tempera and oil paints, mixed with turpentine, the colophony for my violin's bow, and the scent of old books. I can still smell each home I have had, particularly those from my childhood. The smells I remember are like friends to me. I can always call them up, visit them, and trust them. Some of them that is ... Others, by contrast, can actually make me nervous.

Once, when I was in my forties, my husband and I were walking down Chelsea Manor Street in London, where he wanted to show me the home of a friend now dead. Suddenly I was overwhelmed by a smell coming from a window. Before I was able to identify that smell, I felt my grandmother's gentle hand stroking my head. Her small hands were skinny, and I could feel the fine bones in each finger.

She used to live only a couple of houses away from us, and I used to spend much time in her place, another home of mine. I loved staying overnight at my grandparents'. After dinner, my grandmother used to read to me. Not necessarily bedside stories. She was a literature teacher, so she always found some passage from a novel or a short story that was appropriate for me. Then, when it was time for me to go to sleep, my grandparents sat at the small games table in the living room, next to the huge French window, and played their traditional evening round of backgammon. They used to leave the door to the bedroom slightly open, to make sure that I was staying in my bed. I loved the rhythmical sound of throwing the dice and moving the wooden pieces on the board. In wintertime, when it was cold and wet, my grandfather used to prepare a special drink for them to have while they were playing. He heated up *rakia*, a kind of plum brandy, on top of the coal stove and spiced it with pepper, cloves, and honey. The intoxicating scent of this aromatic drink made me drowsy and I would fall asleep hoping to have an amazing dream.

My grandparents were also the people who knew me best when I was a child. We preserve the child in us when we grow up, but there is also a grown-up person in each child – almost from the beginning. My grandparents knew the grown-up person in me, when I was a child, and they respected that person – because they loved me very much. For some reason they saw me as their living dream of the future. Their other big dream was in the past – Italy, where their love stood up for its freedom and its rights. As a young man my grandfather spent a few years living in Naples. He was an actor, and he was invited by an Italian theater troupe to work with them. He loved his life in Naples. He loved Italy – the sun, the music, the language. He acted in Italian and he wrote a few plays in Italian, which the troupe performed in different cities. After he spent a few years in Italy, he was asked to move with another troupe to America. But first he sent a letter to my grandmother, the love of his life. He just wanted to say goodbye, since her mother wouldn't allow her to marry him – a hopelessly moneyless actor. Upon receiving his letter, my grandmother packed a suitcase, did not say anything to anyone, and took the train to Genoa where she secretly married my grandfather. Almost in everything my grandparents loved there was some reference to Italy, even in the abbreviated Italian version of my name – Ditta.

The most memorable smell in my grandmother's house was the smell of fresh sweet fruit preserves. People on the Balkans prepared large amounts of pickled vegetables and sweet fruit preserves for the winter. Not for luxury, but because when I was little, in the winter there were no fresh fruit or vegetables on the market. I remember people standing in line for hours to buy jars of roast pepper or eggplant, pickled carrots, cauliflower or sour cabbage – to stock them for the winter. One could buy jams more easily, however, and my grandmother's generation may have been the last one that felt they should make fruit preserves every autumn themselves.

Originally, sweet fruit preserves were served in a Turkish manner – in small quantities, on a special small crystal plate, much smaller than a saucer, with a small silver spoon, together with a glass of cold water. In some regions, it was customary to serve preserves as soon as someone came through the door to pay a visit – the whole tradition inherited from the Ottomans. This custom was observed especially when members of the groom's family would visit the family of the girl to arrange the marriage. Somehow, as a child, I wanted to belong to the generation of home-made fruit preserves, not to the one of the ready bought jars of jam. I was dying to sit down in grandpa's big armchair, waiting to get the first big sweet prune of the season, stuffed with a walnut, covered with a thick amber-brown syrup, and spiced with rose geranium, served on a crystal plate in the shape of a rose petal – the whole regal thing brought to me on a silver tray. As if I was in a book, one of those about old times that my grandmother used to read to me. A time machine, which always brought me back to the history of my grandmother's family: to her father's country mansion in Sliven, at the foot of the Balkan mountain, where her mother taught the maid how to spice the preserves, while wearing a wide brimmed hat and lace gloves, just before she would go out for a horse ride. Something my mother's preparing of pickled cauliflower on the kitchen table in our apartment in the city could not do for me.

The rite of serving the first spoon of preserved fruit was observed only at the end of a procedure that lasted for hours. In the fall, when my grandmother chose the day for making the preserves, grandfather started the fire in the big cast iron stove. The fruit preserves in the Balkan cuisine are very different from a jam. They are exceptionally sweet, and the sugar syrup is much thicker. The fruit is supposed to remain whole. It should not fall apart. The preserves were cooked on low temperature on the stove, in an open, wide and shallow pan, *tava*. Once the fire in the stove was lit, my grandmother and I started preparing the fruit. We pitted each single prune or cherry, or we cleaned the seeds from the hearts of the quinces. Then grandmother started to boil the syrup. I had to pick a few leaves from her potted rose geranium and to put them in the syrup to aromatize the preserves. When the syrup was thick enough, grandmother added the fruit to it and started stirring the preserves, very slowly, with a long wooden spoon. From time to time, the mixture would produce foam that had to be skimmed. I always had the important task to try the foam and tell Baba (granny) if I thought the jam was sweet enough. After a while grandmother would start checking if the jam was ready. She would let a drop of the mixture fall on a clean and absolutely dry saucer from a clean and absolutely dry teaspoon. The drop was supposed to stay whole and not to spill, as a small colored diamond. I could not wait for that moment to come and I was moving impatiently left and right, looking from behind Baba's back at the intensely colored bubbling foam. That meant that grandmother had to check the shape of the drop often, so that I could get to lick all spilled drops off the saucer. In the meantime, grandfather would usually stand in front of the mirror in the hallway and recite verses from the new role he was going to perform at the theater. Many months after grandmother had made the preserves, her apartment still smelled like cooked prunes and quinces, rose geranium and cloves, mixed with the scent of her old wooden Ottoman cupboard – the scent that came over me that day on Chelsea Manor Street.

Before the war, my grandparents' building, where they had bought an apartment after having sold their house in the outskirts of Sofia, used to have central heating. The pipes were hidden behind the walls. During the war and later, after the communist coup of 1944, people had to give up those central heating systems in urban apartment buildings for lack of resources, and each family had to figure out how to heat their own home. In most apartments there were one or two small coal stoves, and, in addition to the regular electrical heater, a big combined wood and coal stove in the kitchen. Because of that the whole city, like most big cities in Europe, used to smell like coal. Coal was delivered once or twice during the fall and it was kept in the cellars, from where every single day it had to be brought up to the apartments in relatively small tin buckets. I was only six when a modern centralized district heating system was installed in our neighborhood. Nevertheless, I still remember the smell of coal during three out of the four seasons in Bulgaria, and the image of my father carrying buckets full of charcoal up the stairs will never leave me. Today we know that coal was good neither for the environment nor for people's health, but back then I used to love the smell coming from the chimneys. At the same time, I hated seeing my father carrying the buckets with coal. He was the noblest person I will have ever known, and he was old and ill, for he had never recovered from the time spent in a Nazi labor camp as an Ashkenazi Jew. The Bulgarian King Boris III, who was of German descent and formally an ally to Nazi Germany, was the only ruler of an occupied or allied European country who managed to avoid deportation of Jews to the concentration camps and sent them to internal labor camps instead, thus, saving Bulgarian Jewry from the Holocaust.

There have been Jews on the Balkans since the 2nd century B.C.E. Before the 15th century C.E. the largest part of the Jewish community in

Bulgaria consisted of Romaniotes, Byzantine Jews. Most of the Sephardic Jews, however, came to Bulgaria after a major migration wave toward the end of the 1400s when they were expelled from Spain by Ferdinand and Isabella and found a welcoming refuge in the Ottoman Empire under Sultan Bayazid II. The Ashkenazi Jews settled in Bulgaria in several stages. Some of the other known times for Jewish migration to Bulgaria were the years 1376, after Jews had been driven out of Hungary, or 1470 when they had to leave Bavaria. German Jews of my parents' generation had fled Nazi Germany.

My father's father went to Bulgaria for the first time very early in his life, as a *Wanderer*. That means that he walked on foot throughout Europe for years. In the mid-twenties, after he had married my grandmother, a Jewish woman from Vienna, he came back to Bulgaria as a representative of an Austrian silverware company. Later, together with my father, he established a textile business in Sofia and built a couple of factories. My grandparents had five children. The family was travelling back and forth between Berlin and Sofia for about a decade, but all the children went to school in Germany. They spoke German, not Yiddish, and, like most German Jews at the time, they were almost completely assimilated in the German culture. My grandfather died relatively young. My father remained the sole owner and manager of the textile business in Sofia. When in the 1930s circumstances in Berlin became difficult for Jews, my grandmother, her two daughters, and my father decided to settle in Sofia. They felt safe there and it was this very sense of being safe that made Bulgaria home to them. Other members of my family though hesitated until it was too late to escape the Nazis.

In the evening, when the city smelled of coal and wood, my father, one of the fortunate survivors, used to tell me stories from his life, one story every time he sat next to me – until I fell asleep, or until he did.

My mother was not falling asleep that easily. She was a night-owl. She always waited for all of us to go to bed so that she could work in peace. Whenever I woke up at night, our place smelled like paints, usually tempera. My mother was an artist. At night, when I was little, she would take out her palette and start mixing colors. By the morning, the smell of tempera and turpentine had penetrated the curtains, the chairs, the old elliptic dining table, the leather sofa, and our breakfast. In summertime, the smells around my mother were different. I liked them better. We spent most of the summer in our country house. We had many fruit trees and shrubs: cherry, apple, pear, walnut, quince, medlar, black currant, elder bush, raspberries, and what not. One by one the season of each plant would come, and my mother would prepare her preserves. Especially after my grandmother died, my mother felt obliged to prepare supplies for the winter, and maybe, she felt obliged to keep up with the tradition. She used to set a bonfire outside in the garden. She would put a huge cauldron on it and for many days the wind would carry the smell of plum or rosehip, or of elderflower. Sometimes, when I was coming down the hills, after a day in the mountains, the whole village smelled like fruit preserves – my mother was not the only one to make them in the open.

When I think carefully about my sense of home, I realize that the only two places that somehow belonged to me – the first one I rented and the second one I bought – are places I do not remember as my homes at all.

The first one was a nice two-bedroom apartment in Munich. I rented it as soon as I got my teaching position as a lecturer for Bulgarian language and culture at the university. I was preparing complicated and secret plans to assist my first husband in escaping with my older son J., who had remained with him in Bulgaria. I wanted them to be comfortable and to feel safe when they arrived. So, I designated more than half of my salary to paying a very high rent, something many considered a crazy risk at the time. I was happy that I had a job and a good salary. The almost five-year-long period that the law allowed me to teach in Germany as a lecturer seemed to be a very long time and I was confident that I would manage our expenses. Eventually, my older son and his father arrived. Soon after, I started working as an interpreter for refugees from the 1990s Balkan war too. I could not be more fortunate. I could pay the rent, support my family, and even send money to my mother in Bulgaria. I could also afford to furnish the apartment – modestly, but very nicely. I had a custom-made pine wood bed, with shelves over it, for my younger son, a comfortable sofa bed and a desk for my older son, another elegant modern sofa and a round glass dining table in our living room, a bookcase, a TV, and all sorts of gadgets in the sweet small kitchen. For the first time I had my own place and I had arranged it as I wanted to.

Later, after the sudden and unexpected fall of communism, my mother sent me a small transport with some things from home, including my piano. We were happy. However, my sons were treated as foreigners and I realized that this might never change. Then, just under five years after I had started teaching, my contract at the university expired. By law, in Germany a lecturer could have a contract for a maximum of only five years. I did not know that when I signed my contract, but even if I did–I had no other choice. When I was told that I had to leave my job at least for a year, and that it was not clear if I could be re-hired after that, I was scared. I was going to lose everything – again. This was the time when I made a decision to move to America and to try to stay there permanently.

My first husband and I had just divorced. I had custody of both my sons. I also had family in the U.S., and they would not spare any effort trying to help me. My sons and I settled in Minneapolis. However, in the first two years after we moved, I kept my apartment in Munich. I wanted to be sure that if necessary, we could go back – home! I was subletting the apartment, with the permission of the owner, and I was paying the rent regularly. In the middle of the second year, I received a notice from the building management. They broke the lease because someone in the building complained about my tenants being too loud. The apartment was very central, in Schwabing, one of the nicest and most elegant neighborhoods in the city, close to the university and the old city center. I knew that many people wanted to have my place and that some neighbors had asked how it was possible that a refugee from Eastern Europe could have this place. Since I was not there at the moment it was easy to kick me out. All of a sudden, the manager, who had been very kind in the beginning, gave me three months to empty the apartment and threatened that if I did not, they would auction my belongings. Soon after I received that notice I went back to Munich. I had very little time to make any arrangements. A few friends offered to keep some of my belongings for a limited period of time, but I could not find a solution for most of the furniture, for my books, for the family dishes I received from my uncle before he died. To comply with the deadline the building management had given me, I hired a Turkish man, who was willing to pick up the things I had to get rid of and take them to Turkey. One Saturday morning, he came with a small pick-up van. My apartment was on the third floor. I stood at the window and watched the man load my elegant modern sofa, my bookcase, my son's custom-made bed, my clothes, dishes, vases, carpets . . . My successful life of five years was loaded into the van and once again I had nothing left – except for my children. An hour later, I picked up my younger son from his father, we went back to the apartment and we started cleaning. With the dust and our tears, I seemed to have cleaned my sense that I needed to be secure. Nothing in my life was permanent. I learned to lose. This place and this city were no longer home to me. But I knew that the boys and I would pick up the pieces and give our new life the hope it needed. Today, when I look back, I can say that I loved Munich, but in my mind, it no longer occupies the space of a home as other places do.

The second place that I do not remember as my home, was one I actually owned – a house I dared to buy when we lived in Minneapolis. My mother decided to move to a different, much smaller place and sold my father's apartment, where I had grown up. She sent me the money from my inheritance which I was entitled to and I was able to make a down payment on a small house. Since I was a foreigner and had no job, I could not apply for a mortgage with a bank. Thus, I had to accept a private mortgage with the previous owner, and he asked for a very high down payment. So, I invested the better part of what I had in this purchase. My boys believed that this house was going to be our home for the rest of time. They thought we "had made it." J. built almost all the furniture for his room with his own hands. He was just about to graduate from one of the best private high schools in the country, the Blake School, where for a year he was a scholarship student. He had friends, he had an old Pontiac Firebird, which he had always dreamt of, and every weekend he was windsurfing at Lake Calhoun, the beautiful big lake right in the middle of Minneapolis – borrowing equipment from the windsurfing shop where he was working.

I came to Minnesota as an independent researcher at the university. At a talk I gave there, a young woman from the audience approached me and asked if I would consider working for a relatively new company that, after the fall of communism, had started distributing the newly established newspapers and also academic publications from Eastern Europe – mainly to the State Department, the Library of Congress, New York Public Library, and different universities. She believed that with my Slavic languages and my contacts in Eastern Europe, I would be a great asset to the company. I had an interview with the CEO, and I met the charming small staff of about 20 highly qualified, interesting, and enthusiastic young people. I think I fell in love with all of them, as much as I was fascinated by the opportunity I was given. I accepted. My work was interesting. I had to communicate with the major new periodical publications and with academic publishers in Eastern Europe, as well as to make difficult arrangements for getting fresh newspapers from some almost inaccessible areas in the war zone during the 1990s Balkan wars. Soon, I was made Director of the Periodicals Department. My clients were profoundly interesting people from libraries, universities and the State Department and I liked talking to them, though in many cases only via the first, limited version of e-mail available in the early 1990s. My income was miserable. I was paid seven dollars an hour, a little less than friends of mine were paying their teenage babysitter, but that was not the most important thing to me at the time. The company had hired a lawyer who, on their behalf, applied for my green card. I still had a visa that allowed me to stay in the States, but I was paid under the table. However, I had gained more than a job and an income. Some of my colleagues embraced me and my boys as friends. We frequently travelled together – to Lake Superior, to South Dakota, and even to Europe; we visited each other's homes, we celebrated holidays together, and we genuinely cared about each other. I seemed to have settled and my life seemed to be beautiful and fulfilled.

Then, after we had lived in Minnesota for two years, the company I worked for had to downsize. Business was not going as well as expected. I was one of the first people who had to leave. The first thing I asked, when I was told that the company could no longer afford to pay me, was what would happen to the people in my department:

"What department?" said the CEO in a low voice. "You have no people in the department… You have no department… In fact, you are not in the company at all – you do not exist."

As a consequence, my children and I had to give up our home – once again. I realized I should not have bought a house before I had my status sorted out, but I wanted to be independent, and I did not want to overstay my welcome in the house of my cousin's husband, where they had offered us to live while they themselves were spending time in their second home in California. At this point, I was no longer able to make the private mortgage payments. I wasn't sure at all what the next step was supposed to be.

I needed to stay in the U.S. a little longer. My older son was going to graduate from high school in the same year. I had to make it possible for my younger son to graduate too. I needed two more years. It would have been impossible for him to go back to his old Gymnasium, the university-preparatory school he attended in Germany. He had missed two whole academic years and the system was not designed in a way so that a student could pick up where they had left off. My son would have been sent to Mittelschule, a type of a school that ends after 10th grade and that does not qualify students for applying to study at university. For young people with technical orientation, there was the possibility to attend a Technical University, but at that point my son did not seem to be technically oriented. Not graduating would have meant to risk his entire future education and professional development.

I came up with an idea, how I could prolong our stay in the U.S. Before we arrived, I had completed the course requirements in a doctorate program at the Ludwig-Maximilian University in Munich, where I was also teaching. My dissertation was written and accepted by my Doktorvater, my supervisor, but I had not yet taken the last exam – the Rigorosum. So, now I saw not only a possibility for my son to remain in the country until he graduated, but also an opportunity for me to complete the doctorate degree I had started working on in Germany. I applied to a PhD program in German language and literature at the University of Minnesota. I had previously sat in on some of the classes held by the head of the German department and I liked them a lot. It was a real shock when my application was rejected – with the explanation that I was "not qualified to enter a PhD program at that university." *Not qualified?* I wondered. *With an ABD from one of the best universities in Germany, and a previous Master's degree*? I could not think of any other reason to be rejected except that the head of the German department, a German national of the age of my father, might have been an anti-Semite. Perhaps I was wrong but whatever the reason, there was nothing I could do about it.

Meanwhile, I was offered a position by the only competition of the company that fired me. They were in New York and they were interested in my customers contact lists. I had to move to the Big Apple. My younger son was accepted in the United Nations International School. The school year had just started, and I immediately moved him to New York, so that he would not miss much. Then, after I arranged for him to stay with a friend of mine for a few days, I went back to Minneapolis to pack and to drive the car east myself. J., who had already graduated, decided to remain in Minnesota. The night before I left Minneapolis, J. and I were packing the few things we possessed. When we were ready, he said that he couldn't bear sleeping in the empty house anymore.

"I thought this was my home," he said," but it is only another home I have to leave."

That night, he went to sleep in the windsurfing shop where he was working. I stayed alone in our house – the first and last place I bought in my life. Next morning J. and I met for breakfast. Before I started driving to New York, we had to say goodbye.

"Until next time, Mutti," he said, "but we don't know when this is going to be."

This was the second time when J. and I had to part without knowing when we were going to see each other again – the first time was on the day when I escaped from communist Bulgaria. It took me three days to get to New York. The weather was grim. I had to drive slowly and to stop frequently because I could not see much through the windshield. I wasn't sure whether this was because of the rain or because of my tears.

For a few months J. lived in the small room at the back of the windsurfing shop. He continued working there. Once in a while he was also helping in an auto repair shop. We were running out of money and J. was eager to survive on his own. At that point, I was not able to help my child. Things with the job in New York did not work out for me either. One day, a couple of months after I had started working for him, the director and owner of the company came to my office and told me to leave – without touching my computer or taking any files away. He was also able to kick me out of the apartment that he had found for me, because my landlord was a friend of his. My son and I had to move again. I will never know whether the reason for firing me so quickly was the fact that the company already had their hands on my clients list, or because I pretended not to notice the slimy sexual harassment attempts of the director. When I left that office for the last time, all other employees had gone to lunch, except for one honorable man, the deputy director, who stood there, alone, and had the courage to say: "I am very sorry. I couldn't do anything to help."

I found a small apartment only two buildings away from where we lived before. My younger son and I carried our furniture through the backyard, to save money on transportation. I had to sell the house in Minnesota. I lost half of what I had invested in it because of major plumbing problems which were not disclosed by a corrupt inspector at the time I bought it. We lost. We lost what we planned to be our home forever, we lost the American Dream, and we lost the only money I thought I was ever going to have. We believed we had also lost our chance to stay in America. The boys had to be safe. There was no longer a green card application process going on and my visa was going to expire soon. I decided not to take the risk to remain in the country illegally. I told J. that we had to go back to Munich. I was hanging on to the last little money I had, waiting for my younger son to finish the school year, and then I was planning for all of us to return to Germany.

Until that point, I had spent half of my life as a mother alone with my two sons. It was just the three of us. But then my second husband came, my P., a British American. The first one of the three of us he met and got to know was my younger son, who was his student. P. fell in love with our whole family and wanted us to stay together. When he proposed, he proposed to all of us – not just to me. This was how America became our home. Then, years later, after he graduated from College, had a career, got married, bought a home of his own, and had a very sad divorce, J. left that home, us, and the entire continent. "Home" he said once, "is where I live at the moment." I was disturbed when I heard him say this. Did I deprive my children from having a sense of what a home was? Did I deprive them of a sense of identity? Some people have accused me of that, and sometimes I have blamed myself. But the boys have never thought that I have deprived them of the sense of home and of having a sense of identity. I do not believe that either. I think that over the years both my sons have learned to turn every single place where they have lived into a home – their rooms, their apartments, the cities or the countries where they were at any given point. After all, my younger son and I had lived first in Israel, then in Munich, where we were reunited with my older son and their father. Years later, I divorced my first husband, the boys and I left Europe and settled in the American Midwest. After we left Minneapolis and I married my second husband in New York, my younger son lived with us in New York and in his college upstate, then in Cambridge (England), London, Brussels, Paris, Washington D.C., Helsinki, and Oslo, and then again in New York; my older son was back in Munich, then he served as *Feldjäger* (Military Police) with the peacekeepers in Sarajevo – just at the end of the 1990s Balkan War; later he came back to New York, got married, moved to Jersey City, then West Orange, and, after his divorce, he moved to Hong Kong. As a British-American my husband has lived all his life on both sides of the ocean, in New York and in London, and for some time, he lived and worked in Africa as well. Because of him, today I also live both in America and in Europe.

Looking at myself, my children, and my husband, it would be preposterous to say that we have no identity. Just the opposite. We have a very strong sense of identity which, I guess, allowed us to become real world-citizens and to feel comfortable and at home just about everywhere we have lived. Instead of having only one home we have had several. My boys have always insisted that they "would not exchange one day of their lives for any other kind of life." I believe that my grown-up boys place more value on family and on the concept of home than many other people I know. Of course, with time we kept remembering some of the places where we lived as *home* and others we did not. In our turbulent lives, the three of us have learned that the feeling of having a home does not depend simply on one's birthplace or on any other place. Having a home is like having a marriage. It is a relationship. It depends on what a home gives you and on what it deprives you of, but it is something we have to work on. We ourselves have to figure out what we like about our home, why we like it, what we need to do or to change in it so that we like it – we need to establish a relationship to it, a relationship that makes us feel comfortable and safe, that allows us to be joyful, to celebrate, to develop. Home to my sons and me has been a value, a feeling, a belief. It has occupied in the first place a space in our minds – a space we love. That space is shared by a number of physical cities, countries, houses, and even a refugee shelter, but all of them would have crumbled down instantaneously, like sandcastles, if we had not kept alive the idea of home. The primary meaning of the word *refuge* is the condition of being safe and sheltered. Refugees, I believe, are all of us whose condition of feeling safe and sheltered has been thrown out of balance – all of us who have been forced, by different circumstances, to take the excruciating road of the unknown – seeking to restore that balance.

My grandmother

Cogito[18]

My parents' library defined my fragile early knowledge of the world, my dreams, and ultimately my goals, as well as the choice of my profession, and perhaps the better part of my entire life. The four walls of our library were covered with black wood shelves looking at my father's large mahogany desk, with his Adler typewriter, a big old inkpot, and a dip-pen-holder with his golden pen in it. Our library would have been extremely dark and gloomy if it did not have a very wide window looking out on the horse chestnut trees and the sidewalk of the boulevard in front – once the nicest central boulevard in Sofia, Patriarch Evtimiy, named after the 14th century patriarch of the Bulgarian Orthodox Church, patriarch Euthymius of Tarnovo.

Before I learned how to read, some of the most exciting times for me were the times when my father would allow me to go into the library, pick up a book with illustrations, and sit on top of his desk, in one of the corners, looking at illustrations of books, while he was sitting in his brown tufted leather chair with big round brass nails around the edges, working on his translations.

The books were divided into sections. On the very top shelves, which I could not reach by myself, there were Papa's old German books from the late 18th and the 19th century in Gothic script – Lessing, Goethe, Heine, Schiller.... Then, on the next level down, there were my mother's books on history, art history, literary history, her albums with reproductions of works by great artists, of ancient sculpture, of *Art Nouveau* buildings and objects. Then, on the lower levels, there were tons of works of literature and philosophy – ancient, medieval, modern, English, French, German, Bulgarian, American – I always wondered how big the world of our library was. Most of my father's books were in German, English, or French, and those of my mother were in Bulgarian, Russian, and some of them also in German. I had almost no toys to play with when I was a child in the '50s in communist Bulgaria, and I was not much interested in playing with the

[18] Latin. In his *Discourse on Method* (1637) René Descartes made his philosophical statement "Cogito ergo sum," I think, therefore I am.

single old one-eyed doll I did have. But my parents had a lot of time off from taking care of me whenever they would let me sit on top of the desk and look at the original illustrations of *One Thousand and One Arabian Nights* and my mother's big heavy *Iliad*, at albums with reproductions of Goya, Michelangelo, El Greco, or the illustrations to *Gulliver's Travels* or *Tom Sawyer.* These were the most exciting times for me and the quietest times for my parents.

My parents must have been reading to me before I even started understanding what they were reading. Some of my very first conscious memories are memories of Heracles, Hector, and Helen, of Paris and the golden apple contest, of Jason, the Argonauts and the Golden Fleece, and of Aeneas. My mother was reading Greek mythology as bedside stories to me. We had a special edition for children, full of illustrations. I used the same edition to read Greek mythology to my own boys later.

In our family, reading aloud, as a communicative process, did not end with me and my sister having learned to read on our own. We all kept reading to each other – as long as we lived together. I remember when my father had his first heart attack. He was supposed to stay in bed for a long time – maybe a month. During that time, my mother was reading Lion Feuchtwanger's novel *Goya* to him. Later, when I was older, there were days when school was closed or I was sick. On such days my mother, my sister, and I would take turns reading aloud Shakespeare's historical plays, *Don Quixote*, *The Life of Gargantua and of Pantagruel, Tom Sawyer, Uncle Tom's Cabin, The Hunchback of Notre-Dame,* or *David Copperfield*. My older sister was usually reading me fairy tales from different cultures. There was one I made her read to me more than fifty times – I used to count them – *Nal and Damayanti*, a tale from the *Mahabharata*. Usually, I expected my father to read poetry to me – Schiller, Goethe, Byron, because he used to quote poems in a conversation. Whatever we talked about, especially at the dinner table, which was our small-scale home agora, my father found some appropriate poem to quote and I often begged him to read me that poem after dinner. My grandparents also played a major role in my education. I heard for the first time some of the most beautiful Bulgarian poems and short stories from my grandmother. Often, she was disturbed in her reading by my grandfather, who was rehearsing his theater roles in the other room and was too loud in bringing to life his various characters. Sometimes, I did not know whether I wanted to listen to the stories my grandmother was reading to me or to the lines my grandfather was rehearsing.

In an issue from November 2011, *The New Yorker* published an article by James Wood entitled "Shelf Life," based on his personal experience with the library of his father-in-law, Edmund Wilson. The author expressed his doubts that libraries say much about the people who own them. The libraries I have known in my life say everything about the people who owned them – not only in that distant Eastern European world which I left more than thirty years ago, but also in the world I inhabit today.

When I met my second husband, his library was the place where I first realized that I was fascinated with this fifty-two-year-old bachelor. His collection ranged from history and political thought to ancient, European and American literature, poetry, and his own reports from Africa, which he wrote when he was living and working in Tanzania. It is this same library where I am writing this book today, and where I try to spend a large part of my working time. My parents' library formed me as a political thinker, as a writer, and altogether as the person I am. It was that library that, in the midst of an authoritarian regime, made me understand the value of independent thinking, of learning about other cultures and literatures, about the value of education. It was that library that made me realize that I wanted to be free to explore and to study, even if I had to pay a price for having dissident views in a country where intellect was closely controlled and manipulated. I established a profound reverence for libraries, which until today are almost like temples of worship to me – of the worship of human thought, of intellectual development, and of self-expression.

I also wrote my dissertation in several libraries around the world but mostly at the British Library, and I have prepared each one of the classes I taught either at the New York Public library or at one of the Columbia University libraries. My continuous dialogue with authors past and present has been no less important to my life than prayers are to a profoundly religious person, and I have tried to teach my students that future generations will need to stand on the "shoulders of the giants,"[19] who

[19] Part of a famous phrase known mostly as a statement made by Isaac Newton in 1675,

have lived before them as we stand today undoubtedly on the foundation of the human thought carefully engraved on tablets, artfully written on parchment or printed on paper – the documents of our civilization, cleaned, dusted, locked in cases and glass cabinets, and carefully preserved and protected in libraries.

. . .

In addition to my parents' attitude toward the importance of reading, art, music, and generally toward education, there was also a very specific historical phenomenon that formed my views of education. The small country I grew up in, Bulgaria, had been a province of the Ottoman Empire for almost five hundred years – from the conquest of the Second Bulgarian kingdom in1396 to the liberation in 1878 during the Russo-Turkish war. The liberation from Ottoman rule began with the preliminary freedom agreement of San Stefano in 1878. I was born less than a century later. According to the "catastrophe-theory" dominating Bulgarian historiography when I was growing up, an essential part of the Ottoman rule over the Bulgarian provinces or sandžaks was a well-designed and consistent policy of cultural and religious assimilation, despite the existing law of self-government of the Christian Orthodox Church and its communities. The Ottoman policy of cultural and religious discrimination was also aided by the strong influence of the Greek Orthodox Church, which, as people at the time believed, had strived for centuries to prevent an independent Bulgarian Church and to annihilate a genuine Bulgarian culture. Thus, regardless whether this was or was not true, one of the main emphases during the Bulgarian National Revival or Bulgarian Renaissance, aiming at the ultimate liberation of the Bulgarian territories and their national integration, was placed on education. This movement is considered to have started in 1762 with the writing of *Istoria Slavianobolgarskaia,* the *Slavonic-Bulgarian History*, by St. Paisius of Hilandar – a scholar and a monk at the Hilandar Monastery in the Holy Mount Athos. Some powerful tools in establishing what historians call "a national consciousness" included the study of history, particularly of the old Bulgarian kingdoms, as well as building secular schools, publishing

whose concept, however, has been traced back to the 12th century. https://en.wikipedia.org/wiki/Standing_on_the_shoulders_of_giants. Accessed 11/04/2020 newspapers and journals, and sponsoring young men's education in Prague, Odessa, Vienna or Paris. Surprisingly for the time, women were part of this movement too and they often became teachers in the local schools. Having grown up in the family of some of those first well-educated representatives of the Revival, both my grandmother and her sister had completed a Master's degree – my grandmother in literature and her sister in philosophy. Grandmother was a very religious person and I often heard her pray that I would become a good student in school, and that I would learn to love reading and studying. "Literature, history – these are your windows to the world," she used to say. The worship of education – as the basis of civil consciousness, national independence, and the capacity for political self-rule – was the air to breathe when I was growing up, in spite of all perversions in what the communists dictated to be taught in school. I had real reverence for the temples of learning, for universities, and I was in awe of the concept of human knowledge.

No wonder, that when I first started thinking about escaping communist Bulgaria more than forty-five years ago, I was envisioning old universities, where I would be able to study all the literature and all the philosophy that was forbidden or ignored by the regime of my country – Schopenhauer, Nietzsche, Solzhenitsyn, Pasternak and many others, not to mention Rudolf Steiner or any other esoteric philosopher. I was dreaming of libraries where no albums with artworks by great artists such as Salvador Dali or Edvard Munch were going to be locked up in the basement, inaccessible without a special permission that was extremely hard to obtain. I imagined rigorous discussions on democracy or on religion, without whispering and looking over my shoulder to make sure that no one was spying on my views. Most of all, I wanted to live in a world where people were not punished for reading Solzhenitsyn's books, or sent to prison for telling political jokes, a world with no house raids for incriminated literature, with no internments, with no job-deprivation for what the government defined as disseminating Western propaganda – a broad category that was used whenever it was needed, for whatever purpose it could serve.

Many of the students I have taught in Germany and in the U.S. did not know that in antiquity the literal meaning of the notion of *liberal arts* was the study of essential subjects that each free citizen was supposed to have access to, a kind of a study that liberates the mind. I was no free citizen when I was young, and I had no access to those essential subjects. This is why I was dreaming of some place in the world where my mind was going to be liberated. I was dreaming of my Alma Mater. I wanted to escape in order to be free to learn, to think, and to express myself.

More than thirty years later, I became conflicted about my concept of freedom of expression. This concept had been the essence of my existence as a writer – an existence that I identified with since I was a teenager. It also has been the essence of my dreams and my ideals, and it was certainly fundamental for my political thinking. Today, I find myself living in a world that changes rapidly in every possible respect. Technology, science, climate, social media, politics are all areas that reinvent themselves almost on a daily basis. Civilization can no longer see the same image in the mirror two times in a row. In this dynamic environment, we are confronted with threats of various characters too – natural disasters, epidemics, xenophobia, terrorism, revived racism and anti-Semitism, and the insanity of shooting people for no reason. Some of those threats are more clearly related to the way we think than others, though in my mind, there is almost nothing in the world today that is not related to thought, not even many of the natural disasters which are due to climate change. To keep up breathlessly with the pace of change, I try to follow the news on different radio stations and television channels, and I am on social media too.

I spend also about an hour every morning listening to the BBC World Service. I have been doing this since I was seventeen years old, even in Bulgaria where the regime was trying to jam their broadcasts. Recently, there was an interesting program on BBC. A journalist was interviewing young people from different countries on the question of hate speech. Is it dangerous to offer a forum for hate speech? Does hate speech instigate action, including terrorism? Is it right or wrong to take down statements of hate speech from social media, etc.?

The pace of social and political changes in our world has made the fine line between exercising the right to free speech and giving voice to hate speech hair-thin. Does control of hate speech equal infringing on the right to free speech? Who is to be the judge? Would any control mean an authoritarian approach? Would absolute freedom lead to dystopia?

I do not know the answers to those questions. I also believe that it is quite irresponsible for anyone to think that they know the answers, or that there is one clear answer. But there was one question in this broadcast that got two contradictory answers and I was very surprised. Do ideas, thoughts matter? Some people thought that, unless a statement calls for action, ideas or thoughts are "just that – ideas or thoughts," and, thus, they do not matter.

My take on this question may well be biased. I have spent my life studying and teaching the development of ideas and the connection between ideas of different times, cultures, and religions – juxtaposing, comparing, and contrasting them, following the leads from one idea to another, analyzing their transformations throughout time. No culture and no political system have surfaced out of the blue. We have reworked ideas of democracy, courts, or government, born in ancient Greece. The French Revolution worked with ideas of the American revolution and the British political system. Einstein had an idea, before he started developing his theory of relativity. Hitler's appearance was well prepared by the ideas of growing Austrian and German anti-Semitism after World War I. Did his idea of the purity of the Aryan race not lead to action – the mass extermination of non-Aryans during the Holocaust? Isn't every moment before us a nucleus in each moment to follow? Does it not defy any logic to say that ideas do not matter? At some point ideas become the basis of a theory that we act upon – whether we realize that there is a connection or not.

Do I want to have the right to free speech? Absolutely! Do I want my neighbor to have the right to free speech? I do. Do I want to listen to quasi-scientific explanations why black people do not have the capacity to develop intellectually as well as white people? To hear the conspiracy theories about Jews being behind the Central American caravan? To hear a gunman shout in a synagogue that all Jews have to be killed because they are killing "his people?" No! I do not want to listen to such ideas! Not again!

I realize that in the U.S., when proven, incitement to violence is criminal. However, the hair-thin line between preventing hate speech from effecting action and depriving someone from their right to free expression is the tightrope-walking my contemporaries have to do – morally and politically. I am very anxious to see how this earthshaking question will be resolved, but I hope that we will all realize early enough that thought comes before each and every one of our actions.

I am enormously grateful that I have had the opportunity to teach my students independent thinking in classes on ideas, because it gave me the chance to contribute to a generation's awareness of the interconnections of thoughts throughout history and of the power of thinking. Our knowledge of the past is very important with regard to social and political questions, not only in science. What matters most, however, is our attitude to thinking. We cannot and should not separate thought from the essence of creating – for thinking is the first step to any creation. The next step is transforming thought into reality – into a discovery, into a movement, into a construction, and into action. By thinking we reinvent ourselves, our lives, and our world – moment after moment, after moment. Thinking is who we are as humans.

Thinking, and particularly free thought, is also the primary guarantee for the survival of democracy. Social comment is not possible without free thought. It is our very thinking that makes us free. When I think about being free, I am often reminded of Nietzsche's question in *Thus Spoke Zarathustra*: "Free for what?" Certainly, we need to be free for many things – to have property, to make money, to elect our government, to choose our profession, and so on and so forth. But before all that, I think, we need to be *free to think*. This conception has two implications: on the one hand, we need the freedom from interference with our thinking to be regulated by the law. On the other hand, however, real freedom of thought can be achieved only within ourselves, internally, by ever expanding the parameters of our own capacity of thinking. Descartes believed that if we think then, consequently, we exist. But, echoing Nietzsche's question "free for what?," I would like to ask: "think about what?" If our existence really depends on our thinking, then education is our main means to develop the ability to think and to understand the ever more and more complex issues of the time. In fact, we are not free at all if we restrict this ability. Not thinking as much as we can, on all possible intellectual levels, would be as if, all of a sudden, speech is no longer available to us. We would be trapped, enslaved, by our own diminished capacity to think. The Roman poet Juvenal believed that a healthy mind could exist only in a healthy body (*mens sana in corpore sano*) and that there is no healthy body without exercise. I believe that a healthy society consists of healthy minds, and that there is no healthy mind without exercise in thinking. Two great authors, Yevgeny Zamyatin and George Orwell, have painted the nightmare of a world without books and with controlled thinking – the former in his novel *We* (1924) and the latter in his book *1984* (1949). But in 2018 in Kuwait, a country that wanted to promote itself as an enclave of intellectual freedom among its conservative neighbors in the Persian Gulf, a censorship committee at the Ministry of Information issued an arbitrary list of thousands of banned authors, including Dante, Dostoevsky, Goethe, and Garcia Marquez, having read only reports about their works and never the books themselves.

Zamyatin's and Orwell's nightmare, that people will be deprived of their independent thinking and will be given a thought-matrix to model their thoughts upon, became reality once again. What was even more disturbing was the fact that along with the voices raised in opposition to the ban, there were many tweets by individuals who apparently did not like some of the books on the list and agreed with the ban. All this, I thought, has to remind us that thinking is also an enormous responsibility, which, in my view, is often underestimated, even in the free Western world. It is not enough to exercise our minds, to compare and contrast, and to analyze. In some countries, including the U.S., the fact that people have had freedom of speech and freedom of thought for generations has led to a strange phenomenon – the sense that one is also free not to think, not to read, not to be informed. I see this as one of the greatest ironies and tragedies of democracy and of a free society – that freedom makes some people believe that they are free from the obligation and the responsibility to think. This fact, in its turn, allows people to believe in all sorts of nonsense such as fake news and conspiracy theories, or to follow perverse political or religious ideas. Societies that are at risk of oppression seem to have much more avid readers and consumers of news – a phenomenon that appears as a defense mechanism in resisting oppression. Without exercise in thinking we lose the ability to tell apart truth from lies. Without exercise in thinking we cannot and should not trust the thoughts we give birth to.

At conferences and faculty meetings I have witnessed discussions about the importance of teaching humanities, as well as fights over the role of classes on great literature or surveys of philosophy. These discussions have reminded me of my youth, when people were persecuted for studying philosophers such as Nietzsche or for reading works on religious philosophy. When, years ago, while still in Bulgaria, I published the first post-communist-coup translation of a few excerpts from Nietzsche in a relatively liberal newspaper, dozens of students marched into my classroom to congratulate me. "We will no longer be deprived of thinking," said one of them. "This is only the beginning!" said another.

Discussions about the need to teach students independent thinking also reminded me of the Turkish children in Germany of the 1980s and 1990s, and the conscious attempt to prevent them from attending *Gymnasium* – the main path to university. This was an informal way of limiting the intellectual potential of the Turkish population. At the end of the fourth grade of primary school, German teachers were empowered to decide on the educational fate of all students in their classes. Turkish children were more often than not redirected towards either *Hauptschule*, in which they would graduate after 8th grade only, or to the *Realschule*, where they would have an education up to the 10th grade, when they would be allowed to attend a professional school or an apprenticeship affiliated with the guild system, rather than a *Gymnasium* where they could complete the 13 grades (now 12) with an *Abitur* – the requirement for university entry. So, the German school system required teachers to determine whether a child at age 11 should continue on the path of the more academic high school education, or if they should graduate earlier and get some professional qualifications, or maybe, if very bright, go to a technical university. Based on my own experience as a mother of two sons and as an educator, I believe that it is too early to determine the destiny of a person when that person is only 11 years old. However, my point was that, with very few exceptions, Turkish children were prevented from going to *Gymnasium* and thus to University. All this reminded me of the English, French, Russian, and German high schools in Bulgaria, or the so-called language high schools. These schools were accessible mainly, if not exclusively, to young students enjoying the officially determined and recognized "privileges of fighters against fascism." A diploma from one of those schools used to open different doors regarding university entry, jobs, and party membership. Even though the reasons were very different, to my surprise, the German government had also created an inequitable, two-tier educational system, that not only ensured that the highly coveted university spots and consequently the white-collar professions were kept mainly for Germans, but that also had the potential for the social exclusion of minorities.

Since the European Enlightenment, and particularly in more recent history, the role of education in the development of the individual and of civil society has been widely recognized. Du Bois, who fought for equal rights for blacks in the 20th century, saw education as a guarantee that African Americans, who had been emancipated only a few years before he was born, would be able to rise to the level determined by their own capacities. Helen Keller recognized the importance of education for the emancipation of the disabled. Malala believes that the right of all girls to have access to education can change not only Pakistan but the world. And Abraham Lincoln realized the importance of self-education, even where there was little possibility for a formal education. The point, I believe, has always been to have training in profound ways of thinking by learning from the profound thought of others.

The lack of good training in thinking presents a tremendous danger to the formation of political, racial, and religious views and can easily support extremism. Democracy cannot be safe not only without free speech – it cannot be safe without a profound understanding of the responsibility to *think*. Society is based on thoughts and ideas and, thus, citizens must take to heart the responsibility to train themselves in thinking and to see education in thinking as the bulwark of a stable democratic social order.

Our favorite library

Terra Nova

The *New World* is a term created at a particular historical time. We used it centuries ago to describe a world which was new only in relation to another world – the one known to Eurasian history before the discovery of the Americas. Why was it called *new*? Because it had been unknown? Or because it opened the gate to entering dreams? Why was it possible to believe in the dreams of the new world? Because people didn't know what would be impossible there?

Is it that we believe something is possible only when we do not know that it is impossible? Or is it the state of *tabula rasa,* of a blank slate, that makes belief and hope possible? If we have no experience of a world we have never perceived, this allows us to approach it with hope. Try to imagine being able to think in this way about more things in life, not only about a world which we have never experienced. Say, we think like this about a religion we do not know, or about customs we have never seen before, or an ethnic community in whose neighborhood we have never been? But we don't do that. In such cases we tend to think that what's familiar is also what's best and safe. Social experiences we have not had before make us uncomfortable. We are curious and adventurous beings, and we make huge steps towards the unknown in science, but most of the time we hesitate to knock at the door of our Muslim neighbor. Time and again I have heard people who were trying to escape war, persecution, hunger, being called criminals, terrorists, murderers, drug-dealers, rapists. Why were some people seeing that in the march of the caravan from Honduras, in the Mexicans trying to cross the U.S. border, in the Syrians coming to Europe? Because they did not know anything about those people and because they did not want to know? Were there criminals among those in the endless streams of refugees? Were there terrorists, murderers? Perhaps. Were they more than the criminals, murderers, or rapists among the citizens of any of the countries complaining about being flooded with migrants? Who can tell?

The idea of being in a New World has a very particular place in human civilization. It offers the possibility to believe that in that New World everything could be the way we imagine, while in fact this is simply a matter of how the human mind works and not of how any place in the world works. Many things could be the way we imagine them in various different places in the world, but the display of a new, blank slate in front of our imagination, a space that has no mental content yet and that we could gradually fill with the products of our imagination – that is the most beautiful opportunity offered to us when we want to start walking toward a dream.

I escaped communism when I was thirty-three. With me I had one backpack, the younger one of my two sons, and my dream of the New World.

One evening, more than ten years ago, the phone rang, and my older son announced that he was coming to spend the weekend with us in our house in New England. I was surprised. My son was always too busy. On weekends, because of the traffic, the drive to our house takes at least four, five hours. Usually, the boys came to the house only for big holidays – once or twice a year.

My two sons drove up together on the next day. When they arrived, I had already set the table for dinner and I had cooked some of their favorite dishes – I loved being able to do my Mom-thing again, something I didn't have the chance to do very often. We sat around the old English mahogany table that used to belong to my husband's father. As usual, my husband lit the candles. My younger son opened the cupboard where we kept wine, Scotch, and some other liquor for special occasions. He looked at the contents of that cupboard for a while, found a bottle of champagne that some guest must have given us as a house gift, and brought it to the table. I instantly realized that I was going to hear something big, something very important. I grew silent and looked at my older son.

"I came today," he said, "because I will not be able to come here soon again."

I froze.

"I am moving. To the New World. To Hong Kong."

He was thirty-three.

...

I bought my ticket to Hong Kong the day after my son bought his. I felt as if I was in the middle of a storm, of a tornado. For so many years my older son and I had been chasing each other around the world – almost always living in different countries, almost always trying to adjust to the emptiness created by the distance, almost always feeling guilty that we were not together, and almost always being afraid that life might not be going well for the other one. So now, I had to go and see for myself, with my own eyes, what Hong Kong was about, where my son was going to live, how he would settle in a new place once again. I had to know for sure. Most of all, I had to have an image in my head, an image I could hold on to in the long months and years to come, when I was not going to be able to have lunch with him, to go to one of his grill parties, to have him over for Christmas when he would lie down on the carpet in front of the fireplace in our "Little House" in Western Massachusetts. My idea that someday I would preside over the holiday dinners as the doyenne of the family, as a grandma to whom everybody comes from all around – that idea was fading away like the colors of a pastel painting left in direct sunlight. Our house was not going to be that noisy at Thanksgiving any longer, and we were not going to be wrapping every single little jar of jam for Christmas, just because my older son adored wrapping and unwrapping Christmas presents (something I hated because I was always thinking of the trees that had to be felled in order to produce all that paper). The home my husband gave me and my children, after we had wandered around the world for so many years, was no longer going to be home for one of us – my older son.

But J. needed a new beginning – again. The American dream did work for him indeed. He had it all – the degree, the job he wanted, and, after he married, the huge American family of his wife. Both he and his wife made stellar careers and bought a house in New Jersey where, for two years, J. spent every single weekend remodeling this and that. And he loved it all. But dreams could also crumble like sandcastles. What did not work was the marriage.

"It took the judge ten minutes to dissolve a relationship which lasted ten years," my son said, when he called me after the divorce trial. "What now?" – I thought.

J. leaves his mark on everything and everybody he comes close to. He has a very strong personality. He likes to create, to establish, to build, to restructure, to find new ways, new solutions, to help. At this point, he had to find a blank slate for all of that – a tabula rasa of sorts. It was hard for him to re-invent his life using the pieces of the puzzle that had just fallen apart. And he found a way – the way to a whole new world, the New World of Asia.

J's move to Hong King was related also to a big leap in his career. It came in a package with a higher position and a much higher salary. My son had started working when he was twelve. One day, when we were already living in Munich, J., aged 12, came home from school, obviously being in a hurry for something.

"Can you sign these papers, Mom?" he asked hastily and shoved some papers next to the book I was reading.

"What papers?" I asked.

"Well, since I am only twelve, I cannot sign an employment contract myself, so you have to sign that you agree."

I tried not to look at J. before I had digested what he had said. Instead, I looked carefully at the papers, and tried to keep calm, so that we would not start arguing right away. J. wanted to work for a local newspaper agency and deliver their advertisement brochures around the neighborhood. It was a formal employment contract with a phone number and a name of a person whom I could call to check the details.

"How often do you have to do this?" I asked.

"Three days a week, after school."

I knew, if I said no, J. would have found a different way to make money. I was torn apart between a concern for his schoolwork and the admiration I had for his wish to help me at a time which was difficult for me financially.

"You know, you don't have to do this." I said, "I have a job, I teach, I have a good salary, we just have to be careful how we spend the money."

"I want to have my own salary," said J.

I made a decision and I still believe that it was the right one. I decided to respect my son's initiative and to trust him. I signed the contract. In the following few years, before J. turned 16, he was delivering brochures, including when he broke his leg and had to push the little cart with the brochures walking with one leg in a cast; he and his brother were hired by the German TV program *Tele 5* to participate in children's programs; he took a course in windsurfing and, after its completion, was hired as an instructor at a windsurfing school at Lake Starnberg near Munich; and he also used to repair bicycles in a bike shop. Basically, J. enjoyed working. He liked having his own money rather than asking for the usual pocket money which parents used to give to their teen-age children in Germany. He also enjoyed being able to help me, his brother, his father, and even some of his friends. I believe that J.'s genuine generosity was developed in those early teen-age years when he realized that helping others gave him a lot of pleasure and joy.

To J. making money has been primarily a means to help, to offer others certain opportunities. All this does not mean that he is not enjoying his style of life, as well. J. is now married to a beautiful, hard-working woman, a Filipina, who runs her own travel agency and employs people from different nationalities. He has a stepdaughter of mixed race who is a native speaker of three languages, a grandson and a little niece whom he adores and whose education he is dedicated to support; he works on three different continents and helps his large family in the Philippines. J. was born compassionate – no question. But in the West, he also learned something that I find one of the most beautiful aspects of the concepts of freedom and of wealth: the sense of satisfaction one could draw from sharing – from voluntary sharing, of one's own accord. In our turbulent life, we met some people of means who considered helping and supporting those who were less fortunate to be something necessary and good. The three of us worked very hard and we did the best with every opportunity we had. But I can say that we would not have had the life we have today had we not had the help and support of others – in various different forms. My cousin and her husband offered us a home when we first moved to America. Before they were able to take loans and finance their graduate education themselves both my sons received scholarships – the older one in his last year of high school and the younger one for his undergraduate education. The support came from private individuals. These generous people did not even want us to know who they were, but I kept insisting that we meet. The two families who helped me educate my children, and thus gave them the chance to pursue their happiness, are among the most modest, kind, and warmhearted people I have known. In the first place, however, it was my husband, who, without having that much himself, found profound satisfaction in giving us the chance to follow our dreams. I still consider that learning to share by choice is one of the major advantages of living in the free capitalist Western world.

For a long time, I did not see the other side of the coin. I was neither blind nor an idealist – I was just fortunate to have seen first the best side of America. Today, after I have lived more than a quarter of a century here, I still cannot reconcile in my mind the obvious contradictions between the high ethical standards that American democracy, the idea of social liberty, and some aspects of education can inspire, with the vulgar passions of greed, prejudice, intolerance, exploitation, and self-aggrandizement that surround us, corrupting institutions, society, politics, and most of all, the human being as such. Despite this realization, however, I still firmly believe that the ethical values, the decency, the open-mindedness, and the concern with others, demonstrated by many in all walks of life, are deeply rooted in the notions of freedom and democracy that have been the foundation of the very existence of this country. This decency, open-mindedness, and concern with others, I believe, will always prevail – as long as there is freedom and there is democracy.

J.'s favorite spot

Saying goodbye

With J. in Taiwan

Walking on Dreams

It is quiet in the winter afternoons at the *Tayelet*, the promenade along the beach in Tel Aviv. My son and I used to go down to it to dream, as if it was some sort of a temple of dreams to us. My son was eight back then. He first realized the role of the *Tayelet* in our life. We walked and walked, not quite to Jaffa, but along the better part of the Tel Aviv coast. Or we sat down on a bench and watched the sun setting in the sea. Not an ocean. The Mediterranean Sea is different – it feels somewhat closer, it whispers, it does not shout; it is caressingly warm, and it is green in the winter afternoons. Every now and then, there was a jogger or a passer-by with a dog. But for the most part the *Tayelet* belonged to us. It was ours because we loved it, and we couldn't do without it. We had to dream. We had nothing else. We were living in a *beth olim*, an asylum home for newcomers. We had left our home, our family, our books, my violin and the piano, my son's toys, and we knew nothing about the world in which we had ended up: a world of history and myth, of refuge, and of the first intifada. We were aware of this world, but we had no idea what to do with it – as if we were new-born and we couldn't speak. About a month after our escape from Bulgaria we were full of fears again, full of questions. We had no plans, no money, and not enough clothes. We had no life yet, except that we were alive. But we had the *Tayelet*, in the late winter afternoons.

When I took my little boy and left communism, I left the regime, the conspiracy of lies, the incriminated texts and thoughts, the prohibited words – but also my family, my job, my friends, my home. I was nobody now. A woman with a child. My son was nobody too. A little boy with his mother. We had no merit. We could not claim that we would contribute to anything in any country of the world. "Look at the sea," my son said once at the *Tayelet*. "Don't you see what we will be?" What was I seeing? Where? Myself, determined and happy? In the sea? Or in his eyes? "Let's talk about *some day*!" he said. "It will be great, and papa and my brother will be with us again, and you will buy me toys, and you will be teaching again, and I will be going to school, and we will be living in a big city by the sea… " And I could see. He made me see. I knew. What did that mean? How could I have known? I had no clue. It was a dream. A strong, powerful dream, and we were dedicated to it. What is a dream? To wish? To fantasize? To envision? A mystery? To know, despite the fact that you do not know? A voice of the divine? Not the kind of dream Freud discussed but the vision one has in the mind, a vision one loves. Was this my memory? Was I wishing for the things I knew will happen, or did I know that the things I wished for will happen?

"Let's imagine," my son said, "that it is twenty years later, that *someday is today*!"

This is where he began – with how it would be *someday*. We dream so much and call so many things a dream. That dream, the daydream of my son was green. It was like the sea – endless, deep, it had a voice, it had color, and the horizon was as far as he could see. His brother was always with him in his dream. He had his brother back. Today, they just came back from a trip to Bali, Thailand, China. They laughed together, playing with a tiger, and they rode an elephant. They stood at the Great Wall and remembered their first trip together, sneaking out of home without permission, going to a lake that was a few miles away. Adventurers? That they have always been. In life and in their dreams. Did I know all this back then, at the *Tayelet*? Yes, I think I did. The late American esoteric philosopher Dr. Wayne Dyer says: "Think from the end. That is, assume within yourself the feeling of the wish being fulfilled."[20]

. . .

I learned dreaming, among many other things, from my violin. For years, music was my world, my dream, and my goal. My parents never had to make me practice. Just the opposite. Whenever I did something bad my mother threatened to take away my violin. This was the worst punishment for me.

I got my first violin at the age of three. My sister, who at the time was ten, had started taking music lessons. When she was practicing, I used to sit at her feet on the floor, and I sang along the melodies she was learning to play. Every time she took a break, I grabbed her violin, and tried to play myself. To make me leave my sister alone my parents decided to buy me a violin too. I was still so small that even the smallest size of a violin,

[20] Dr. Wayne W. Dyer. *The Power of Intention*. Hay House, 2004. p. 58

a quarter, was too big for me. But my mother found a violin maker who agreed to create a custom-made violin, especially for me – an eighth. When it was ready, it looked like a toy. The violin maker was an older man with a deep bass voice. I was told that he was famous with his violins, which brought him international awards and reputation, and the title *Master of the French guild of luthiers.* This man, who was a magician in my eyes, had to be certain that all measurements for the tiny little instrument were really correct. Thus, I was involved in the whole process of making the violin from the very beginning. Together, we chose the little piece of pear-wood that was to become my magic friend. I saw him hollow the inside and arch the plates, I watched him carve the scroll, and coat it with the tinned varnish. I got to hold one end of the strings when he first fitted the bridge. Then he gave me a bow, and we had to make sure that the sound post was in the right place. As in Italian, the language from which Bulgaria had borrowed almost all musical terms, the Bulgarian word for the sound post was a diminutive of the word for soul – *dushichka.* I learned that the sound of the violin depended mostly on its soul, and that this fine little piece of wood inside the violin should never be moved. It had to stand straight, in a very particular place, between the bottom and the top plate, and it was not supposed to fall. Therefore, I was supposed to treat my violin with the greatest care, to always put it down carefully and slowly, right into its case, and to never drop it on the floor. Can you imagine the mystery when I got the first sound out of my violin, which had been a piece of raw wood just a month earlier? I was so young back then, and I could not comprehend how all that magic worked. To me, my violin was something with a soul, something living. I never thought that I was playing the violin. In my child's mind playing was something that my violin and I did together, with the help of some mystical force.

I lived with my violin for nineteen years. As a child, I was spending most of my time alone, in a room with closed doors, lest I disturb everybody else at home when I was talking to my violin – sometimes for hours, until I got from her the response I wanted. It was a common undertaking – my violin and I had to produce a voice, many voices, the music I played. In Bulgarian the word for violin is feminine. So, whenever she, the violin, did not want to do something I expected, it was because I did not know how to get her to do it. Whenever something did work out, it was she who had helped me do it. My practice at home, my stage performances, any moment when I had my violin in my hands, represented continuous dialogues between me and the deeper me – my music. When later, as a teenager, I started climbing mountains, I had already learned from my violin that one could make things happen. The most brilliant bits in my musical interpretations were always the result of long hours of work, of repeating the same passages over and over again, of accepting that it did not sound well yet, and of never giving up trying, until it did work. This is how I learned from my violin that dreams could come true indeed.

...

Yet... not everyone's dreams come true. It took me more than two decades to understand how privileged I was. With all the hardship and all the sacrifices, and all the risks, and all the fear – at the end of the day I realized that I was privileged and – more – that I was blessed... because I got to live almost all of my dreams. And I got to live almost all of my dreams not only because my sons and I were strong, hard-working, and persistent, but also because of those who helped us, because of those who supported us, because of those who did not deprive us of the right to pursue happiness. I could have never gotten where I am today without the help of other people, without their trust and faith in me.

I firmly believed in the possibility to live one's dreams ... Until the day came when boats full of migrants started capsizing off the coasts of Italy, Libya, or Greece and thousands of mothers, fathers, and babies drowned – reaching for the hopes they had from under the bottomless waves of the sea... Until we sent the army against the caravan from Honduras, headed through El Salvador and Guatemala into Mexico... Until men, women, and children fleeing the most horrific war regions were denied the right to stay away from the bombs, the shootings, and the hunger... Until a whole generation of human beings who had grown up in the country of my hopes, who had run and played in the home backyards of America, who had laughed in its schools and cried in its hospitals, who had studied at its colleges and volunteered at its soup-kitchens – until an entire generation of Dreamers was about to be denied the sacred right to pursue happiness...

Until the land of dreams threatened to raise a wall between the world of want and our world of plenty.

I had risked my life and the life of my children, when I escaped through several borders, because that sacred right had been denied to me by a communist regime and I was not going to allow my sons to be denied the right to pursue their dreams and their happiness. What would have become of me if the world on the other side of the Iron Curtain had denied me that right? What would have become of my sons? Of my unwritten books? Of my beliefs? Of my yet untaught students?

Night after night I watch the current news and I listen carefully to the discussions on DACA, on the caravan from Central America, on building a wall at the Mexican border. I hear that immigration should be based on merit only and I ask: What about the merit that can develop under particular circumstances, perhaps with the help of another, the merit that comes with a different education, with a different kind of life? What about offering chances? What about those who have proven to have merit but do not have the documents to go with them?

And what about the tremendous force of creativity that only the motivation of having a dream can give us? I had not escaped a war, or hunger, or disease. I escaped an ideology I could not cope with. I escaped because I had beliefs and values, and I trusted that there was a world where one is free to dream. At the beginning, after I escaped, I was not able to offer the world much merit. But in the years since, I have changed some lives, I have changed my students' views and attitudes, and I believe I made them better citizens. The Little One, my son, who back then crossed all those borders with me, has been working on peacebuilding in postwar regions, on the rule of law reforms, and on security issues around the world. In the late 1990s after my other son, J., had already completed his mandatory military service in Germany, he volunteered to go to Bosnia as a part of a military police contingent with the NATO peacekeeping troops. He said he wanted "to do some good, to help people establish a free, peaceful society." Later, when he was already in the U.S., he helped run a charity for teaching skills to children from a low-income neighborhood in New York. I am grateful for the kind of people they became. Following the news makes me think of the refugees of different times. I think of my father who escaped the

Nazis by finding refuge in Bulgaria. I think of my children and myself, and I wonder – are we all part of what President Trump compared to a "snake" of criminals and invaders, of "animals," as he called them, who "cut people in little pieces … and want them to suffer?" Or are we all part of the endless caravan of people who have always searched for a better life that can mean so many different things for each one of us? What has become of the idea of equal opportunities? Will the boat of my hopes, my trust, and my belief, eventually capsize – just before the coast of my aging life, and will it sink under the bottomless waves of human ignorance?

What often scares people in other people are the things that are different from what they know – *otherness*, different customs, different behaviors, different religious views and rituals, even different accents. The mind develops through experience, education, religion, work, and in many other ways. What I find particularly important in this development are the processes of comparing and contrasting, and of contextualizing, as they give one the ability to understand *otherness*. It is one and the same person that has to understand Machiavelli and Gandhi, Dr. Martin Luther King Jr. and Mussolini. And it is one and the same person who has to understand an evangelical and a Muslim, a liberal, a Democrat, and a Republican, you and me, the elderly and the teenager, and also the exhausted mother from the caravan coming from Honduras. Thus, it is not the discussion of one particular topic or the study of one particular subject, not the reading of one particular author, or of one particular newspaper or scripture that determine the expanse of one's mind. Rather, it is the study of many different things, of many different texts – it is the ability to learn about the other.

…

Some cultures have tried to put the emphasis on the similarities between people rather than on their differences. The Hindi greeting *namaste*, for example, implies greeting God or the divine in each other. Yet, it seems to be easier for people to see first the differences, the *otherness*. I have been wondering for many years now what makes us accept or reject the differences between us.

The first country I lived in for a longer period of time, after I escaped from Bulgaria, was Israel. My younger son was only eight when we arrived there. He could not say a word in Modern Hebrew and originally had no idea what his teacher or the other kids in the class were saying. But somehow, he got excited about the things they were excited about, he fought their fights, he laughed at their jokes, he was invited to play with them both in the school and in their homes. He did not have to struggle integrating. He was part of the world around him. I never understood how children do this, but I have come to believe that there is something more than language, something more than culture or religion. Beyond the contours we draw to describe our so-called identity there must be something else – being a child, perhaps feeling human – sharing a moment, a piece of bread, a smile, some danger. Just look at children playing with other children and you will see that we are more than political, cultural, and religious creatures using language. Observing my younger son taught me that.

Yet, looking at both my children over the next few years taught me also that different societies, different social groups, and generally different social environments, leave their imprint on children's fragile psyche and form their sense that people are different indeed. The same child who initially did not need any particular adjustment after he was torn away from his family, his home, and the entire environment he was used to, my younger son, had a difficult time adjusting in a society where he was treated as a stranger, as a foreigner. We had moved to Germany. When my son entered third grade in the local primary school in Munich, his teacher kept refusing to repeat questions he had not fully understood the first time and didn't do anything when other kids bullied him for failing to speak correctly. She insisted that he should be moved to an *Ausländerschule*, a school for aliens, since he was not going to go to a *Gymnasium* anyway. She was the person whom the German government had empowered to decide my child's fate – once he reached fourth grade – to decide which educational track he would be able to pursue. I decided to move my boy to a different school.

Luckily, his next teacher in the school I moved him to was warmhearted, soft spoken, and eager to make sure that all the children in his class felt comfortable. Nevertheless, we became aware of being treated as *different*. Perhaps I was accepted as German, because of my German origin and because German was one of my two native languages. My older son too was subject, if not to discrimination, then at least to the demonstratively prejudiced attitude of some more or less xenophobic people. Being an outstanding student and being liked by his classmates, he was elected as class-representative in his *Gymnasium* (high school) council. At some point, the parent association had a meeting about an important question: whether an abusive and incompetent Math teacher should be fired or not. One of the parents quoted a statement my son had made in front of the school council, but another parent objected: "We do not need an alien to run our kids' show," said he. No one contradicted him. Years later, when we were living in Minnesota, at the age of seventeen, J. was excluded again from his natural class-community – this time not by xenophobes but by some young spoiled nouveau-riche class snobs, who looked down on him because he was the only scholarship student in a school full of rich kids. Many of his classmates drove all sorts of fancy cars to school. At first, I was driving him to school, but even his ten-year-old Pontiac Firebird I bought him later did not prevent his classmates from making condescending remarks about his car. A girl, who might have liked him, was part of a group of students using drugs. J. realized that at a party in her home, to which he was invited. He rejected the invitation to try some drugs and left the party. From that point on he had to eat his lunch in the school cafeteria by himself. The moment he would join other kids at a table, they would get up, move to another table, and leave him alone. J. had a hard time. He was used to being liked and respected, but now he had to earn his equal place in another new society, yet again.

Otherness, however, can encourage both exclusion and inclusion. At the very beginning when we arrived in Minnesota, before J. received a scholarship at The *Blake School* and my younger son was accepted in a very good public high school, *South-West*, I had enrolled both of them in the pre-IB program at *Patrick Henry High School*. I loved the faculty there – an amazing group of well-educated, interesting, and open-minded teachers who played a significant role in my sons' education. *Patrick Henry* was a magnet school and diversity was one of its key goals. It was located at the border of a low-income black neighborhood and a lower middle-class white neighborhood. From my sons I learned that white and black kids had separate lives in the school: they ate in separate parts of the cafeteria, and they played in separate groups during the breaks. Apparently, there were some unspoken segregation rules, and despite all efforts to organize talent shows and sports events, there was nothing the racially and ethnically diverse faculty could do about it. The rejection went both ways: the white kids didn't want to deal with the black kids and vice versa. In the very beginning, my sons were even asked once why they were going to a school for black students. Gradually, however, the black children in *Patrick Henry* accepted my younger son and literally adopted him. They played with him and he sat at the same table with them at lunch; the black neighborhood kids also accepted him, and they visited our home and played basketball with him in our backyard.

I was not close enough to these kids at the time and I could never ask anyone, why my son was among the few white kids in the school they accepted to be sitting next to them – only one of my sons, not both. Years later, my son explained this to me. He believed they felt that, like them, he was different from the other white kids, because he was not American, and he barely spoke English when he arrived at the school. He was an outsider too, and not like the other white kids. At first, he didn't understand the implicit rules of segregation at all. He took the school bus from the black neighborhood and sat with the black kids not realizing that there might have been a problem with that. This brought him closer to their group than most other white kids.

I found my son's explanation fascinating. To me, it meant that the pretty open segregation in *Patrick Henry* was not really based on racial prejudice. Most likely, it was based on social and behavioral prejudice. *Otherness* played a major role in distancing the two racial groups, but it was also the basis for the bond the black kids created with my son, a phenomenon seen many times in history when Jews and Muslims would support each other against the persecutions of Christians, or in other similar cases.

I have always thought that if we learned more about the *other*, if we got to know those who are different from us, if we were familiar with other cultures, religions, or customs, we would do much better not only understanding or tolerating one another, but actually living with each other. Many share this ideal, and it has been one of my dreams to see it realized in life – one of the few unfulfilled dreams of mine.

In 2012, after the *Sandy Hook* shooting, I tried to organize a small interfaith and intercultural group in the small town in Western Massachusetts where we have our house and where I do most of my writing. I invited a Tibetan woman who was Buddhist, a Muslim friend of ours and his young son from Florida, a local priest, and a few other people. My invitation to them was provoked by the spontaneous need to share our feelings about the killing of innocent children and their teachers. However, I also thought that our diverse local community provided a great opportunity to raise and study different questions about culture, religion, gun control, and many other issues – an opportunity to listen to one another.

"But I do not wish to be with people who are different," objected a friend of mine. "I want to be with like-minded people."

The group failed. I was not strong enough to make the other people in it overcome this perspective, even though I tried to defend my point. This was a very sad disappointment. *I'd better write about those issues*, I thought. Six years later, in 2018, eleven Jews were shot dead during the Sabbath service in the *Tree of Life* synagogue in Pittsburgh.

"All Jews should die," said the perpetrator during the investigation. "They are going to kill my people."

Gregory Bowers seemed to be a monster … insane. But what was he talking about? What did he know about Jews – from his town or about any other Jews? I could not help recalling the rhetoric of our time – Mexicans described as criminals, drug dealers, and rapists … The threat that the people of the caravan from Honduras were going to invade our country … Did this rhetoric create an atmosphere of aggression or did it result from an existing atmosphere? I cannot say. What I am wondering is how much we knew about the people from the caravan? And why did many people refuse to learn anything from the epic reports of the journalists? History repeats itself, says the cliché. In my personal life as an immigrant in different countries it has repeated itself indeed. I am thinking again of the statement of a Bavarian *Bundesamt* official I already quoted, who believed that the refugees from the 1990s Balkan Wars should not be sent to small communities lest the foreigners start looking more human to their German neighbors and it becomes more difficult to get rid of them. "Love thy neighbor!" we are told. But who is the neighbor? Or do we get to pick and choose, and to edit the Scripture?

Difference is the brandmark of nature as it is known to us. We are all different from each other. Some differences are noticeable, and some are subtle. In the endless masses of people migrating around the world we may not be able to tell apart a criminal and a murderer from a worker, a doctor, or a teacher. We would be able to tell them apart only if we knew them. The question of controlled migration is very complex, and I would never pretend that I know the answers. Yes, I agree that there are tremendous risks involved in letting everyone go wherever they want. I am not a politician and I do not know how to solve that problem. But there is one thing I am certain of: Having dreams is the most precious merit humans have. Dreams make us strive, they make us strong and resilient, they make us develop, progress, achieve, and heal. People who have dreams do have merits. Dreams, like faith, are the basis of strength. A space where dreams do not exist is futile, and a person with no dreams is unproductive. Dreams have advanced human thought – in science, as well as in society. It is dreams that can make people and countries great. The history of our civilization is both a history of dreams and of horror. I ask: what will we be left with if we have no more dreams?

...

My sons and I – we have been living our dreams. With time those dreams have been changing. They may have grown smaller or bigger, but we kept living them. Did all of our dreams come true? Not all but most. How was that possible? My guess is that we ourselves were our dreams and our dreams were us. They were the stuff that made us up and, thus, they made up our lives. Was that a blessing, a gift from above, or was it our choice? What were the means that allowed us to live the dreams we had? Perhaps, we have been strong, determined, fortunate, and blessed – all of the above! I cannot tell. But today, having lived the life I have, I can say that for one to achieve any dream, or any goal for that matter, it takes the hearts, the minds, and the courage of others too. For me, to be the person I am today and to have the life I have, it took more than just me – it took the work of all of those who helped and supported me. That day in Rome, eight years ago, when my younger son and I celebrated a quarter of a century since we escaped, I was looking at the Pantheon, the temple of all gods, with its amazing dome gathering the rays of sun and moon, as if to focus them on the enormous capacity of the human mind – the human mind that, however, is impotent if it stands alone in an isolated space – without the treasure troves of the past, without the diversity of the beliefs of others, and certainly without the efforts of people working in concert with each other.

Punting in Cambridge

Da Capo.[21] Epilogue

I find myself frequently thinking about the fact that I have learned how to dream from my violin, and how to have faith and to survive from trekking in the mountains. Soon after I escaped from Bulgaria a very close friend in Israel said to me that I must be either incredibly brave or really crazy. I think I was neither. I feel quite silly when someone points out my courage because I have never been sure if I had any courage at all or, perhaps, I never realized what kind of courage I had. I have been scared, afraid, concerned, discouraged, even desperate – all of it. But it is true that I have never given up my dreams, the goals I believed in. Sometimes, I have felt alone, rejected, abandoned when walking on the path I had taken. The world around me had seemed unresponsive, unkind, hostile. At times, the ideas, the practical goals I have had kept moving away from me as the horizon moves farther and farther away while we think that we are getting closer. In all those moments, the mountains, that have been always part of me, reminded me of how to walk, of how to survive, and of how to continue on the path. My vivid body-memory has always reminded me of walking downhill into the safety of the valleys, and of walking uphill toward the unknown. So many times, the meditative state of focusing only on one single step at a time has preserved my strength and my ability to keep my balance when moving along the edge of an abyss, to walk despite strong winds which have pushed me down, to cross vast expanses of rock mountains or of snow-deserts, where one could lose perspective and the sense of space and time.

I wish I could share those experiences with all who choose a road of unknown slopes. To my brave and courageous or scared and discouraged fellow dreamers, to my fellow refugees and migrants and to all my fellow men and women I could offer a small gift of an image – the image of walking in the mountains, above the tree-line, where there is nothing else but you, the planet, and the universe. Go there – in your mind or in reality, and you will never lose your faith.

...

[21] Italian. Musical term giving directive to start again from the beginning of a section or of the entire piece.

In 2013 I was again in the Himalayas. This time I had chosen to do the Sandakphu trek. The route repeatedly crosses from India to Nepal and back – something I certainly was not aware of in the mountains, except at the checkpoint where I had to get my Nepalese visa. I chose this trek for two reasons. In the first place it begins in Darjeeling, a city I had visited before but wanted very much to see again. In addition to its spectacular location, Darjeeling is home to the Tibetan Refugee Self-Help Center established in 1959 by some of the first refugees who escaped from Tibet following the Dalai Lama. The Center was created in order to support the Tibetan refugees who organized themselves believing in the principle of self-help, of becoming completely independent in a foreign country. The first time I had visited Darjeeling I met a woman from Tibet, Diki, who owned a wonderful small Tibetan restaurant on Gandhi Road, right next to the old Dekeling Hotel, owned also by a woman from Tibet. Diki was deeply involved with the Tibetan Refugee Center. We became friends and she had promised to introduce me to the work of this amazing organization the next time I would come. Darjeeling is also home to the Everest Museum and the Himalayan Mountaineering Institute. I had been following the history of the attempts to climb Mt. Everest since I was a teenager. I had read about the successful expedition of Edmund Hillary and Tenzing Norgay in 1953, and in 1984 I had bitterly cried over the death of the first Bulgarian who climbed Mt. Everest, Khristo Prodanov – alone, without oxygen, and choosing the most difficult route through the West Ridge. Khristo disappeared on his way down from the summit. For someone like me, who has always been fascinated with mountains and with mountaineering, visiting the Everest Museum in Darjeeling, seeing the photographs taken during several of the Everest expeditions, the books that belonged to some of the most famous mountaineers, a letter written by the first person to attempt climbing Chomolungma, George Mallory, and some of the equipment these exceptional people used – their backpacks, hats, gloves, their compasses – seeing all this was important to me, for in my mind this was able to get me as close to the highest peak on earth as I was ever going to get. So, starting a trek in Darjeeling gave me the great opportunity to see the Everest Museum and to visit my friend Diki and the Tibetan Refugee Center.

The most important reason to choose the Sandakphu trek, however, was different. Sandakphu is the highest peak in West Bengal. If the weather cooperated, from there I could see the tallest peaks in the world – Lhotse, Makalu, and Everest itself on one side, and the Kanchenjunga range consisting of twelve peaks that together form the so-called Himalayan Sleeping Buddha. I knew it was too late for me to be able to climb any of these amazing peaks, but I had to see them – at least once in my life.

Despite the strong objections of my sons, I decided not to join a group but to go on this trek alone – only with a mountain guide. I wanted this to be my time, without much talking, without having to consider the different abilities, moods, and characters of other trekkers.

I met my guide a few days after I arrived in Darjeeling. He was a young, unexperienced man, and he had just started working for the trekking company, Aqua Terra, which had already organized a few of my previous treks in the Himalayas. I gladly accepted working with him because he was one of the Tibetan refugees in Darjeeling and he had a family and a small child. So, I knew that the fee I would pay for the trek would help indeed.

Everything seemed to be going well. We booked a private car to take us to the Nepalese border where I was supposed to get a visa, and we hired a Sherpa who was going to carry my second piece of luggage, but who was not going to be walking with us. I was fascinated with the beautiful, well maintained, and exceptionally clean Nepalese villages we stayed in during the first few days. Then the day came to take the trail to Sandakphu.

My guide advised me not to take much food in order to walk with a lighter backpack. He insisted that there were two places on the way where we could get tea and noodles. I listened to him and I took only two energy bars with me. On the way, however, the weather suddenly changed, as it often happens in high mountains. The cloudy sky was getting darker and darker and the wind started pushing against our faces. Soon it started snowing, as I originally thought. Actually, what was falling down were soft pellets of hail. It became difficult to find the trail under the white cover. My guide seemed to be concerned about the Sherpa. He asked me to stay put for a few minutes in order to go look for him. I did. The few minutes turned into half an hour, and then into forty minutes, and I started getting cold and nervous. After almost an hour had passed, I realized that my guide had lost me. I had no chance to find my way by myself. However, I had some experience in looking for footprints in snow and I decided to try to follow him. It was very difficult to find his tracks, but it was not impossible. I tried to leave very good footprints myself, so that I could find my way back if necessary. It was not necessary. In about twenty minutes I found my guide who was now looking for me and had not found the Sherpa. I said I was not happy that he left me alone in the storm, we agreed that he was not going to do this again, and we continued walking toward the first place where we could have a shelter and a cup of tea. It was closed – probably because of the bad weather.

When you trek in the Himalayas you constantly have to go up and down bigger or smaller hills. Before we were supposed to climb up to the teahouse that we were going to stay in at Sandakphu, we first had to go down for a while. It was getting colder and the pellets of hail were somewhat harder now. I put on my woolen hat and the hood of my rain poncho–to protect my head. I had excellent rain gear, but, stupidly, I had forgotten to take my gloves out of the bigger piece of luggage that went with the Sherpa. I was used to walking with snow poles, which at this point I really needed, in order to feel more stable and to keep my balance. Thus, my hands were outside the rain poncho, holding the snow poles. After a while my skin started cracking – from the cold and from being hit by the ice pellets. Then some of the cracks started bleeding.

After seven hours of walking, we reached the second shelter where we could have had tea. It too was closed. I was hungry and my energy bars did not help much. The sun must have been setting – it was getting darker. We started another ascent. I realized that my energy was very, very low. I was walking much slower now. In a hasty voice, my guide explained that if he were alone, he could walk faster and bring help – someone who could take my backpack, since he was carrying his own and could not help me. He said he might even be able to bring a sled and pull me up to the tea house. We had gotten to a part of the trail that was leading directly up to the tea house and that was quite clear. I let my guide go ahead and bring help. He left.

The hail had not stopped yet. Being now absolutely alone, I tried to pull myself together and to walk with robust steady steps – I had to reach the tea house. This did not last very long. I couldn't stand the weight of my backpack any longer and each step took me some effort to move my legs. I did not feel my hands, so I folded my snow poles and put my hands inside my pockets, under the rain poncho. Walking without the snow poles became even more difficult and certainly slower. I was not seeing very well either. I wear eyeglasses but I had not prepared glasses for winter conditions. My lenses were fogged and the wet drops on the outside were probably freezing too. I tried to take them off but could not see what I was stepping on, so I put them back on.

I had walked now about nine hours and there was no tea house to be seen on the horizon. I felt very sleepy and wanted to sit down and rest. I knew I should not do this. It would have been the end. *But it might help*, I thought. *I am so tired.* For a moment, I thought that I had fallen asleep while walking. I believe I did. *Don't fall asleep, just don't fall asleep,* I kept telling myself. But my entire body had fallen asleep. I did not feel my legs, even though I was still moving them; I had no sensation in my hands, in my face . . . . The night was falling – heavy, freezing cold, and merciless. I knew – this might be the end. There was nothing I could do about it, nothing to fight against, nothing to prevent things from taking the course they were taking. And there was no one else – just me.

Today, looking back at this moment, I find it very interesting to recall what my thoughts were like, how I behaved. There was no drama. My thoughts were slowing down the way my body was. But they were not chaotic, they were only much simpler. I felt no fear, maybe because fear requires some energy and I had none left. Strangely, I found the circumstances quite appropriate to me. What better place to fall asleep forever than the mountains, the Himalayas – the big love of my life!

The feeling I most clearly remember having at that time was the feeling of humility. I was quiet, and peaceful, I was slow, small, powerless, helpless, and this was it and it was fine . . . . There was no one around to give instructions to, no one to apologize to or to forgive . . . no one to say farewell to. It was just me, the road, the dark sky, and the white hail. But God, whom I have loved all my life and who has loved me all my life–God was there. So, I was not alone after all. I was content . . . I had surrendered . . .

Then suddenly I thought that I was seeing something like a building in the distance. I took my glasses off to dry them and the thing I had seen disappeared. But when I put them on again, it was there. Very far away, on top of a high hill, there was a roof and there were some windows… yes, there was a building. *It must be the tea house*, I thought. It took me some time to get out of the state of peaceful lethargy I was in, but not much…. I thought of the two other times when I could have vanished in the mountains but survived. *I can survive,* I thought, and kept repeating it to myself, *I am a survivor, I will survive…*

In a few minutes I started walking somewhat faster again. First, I felt only my heart beating, but then I felt my legs and my hands as well. I had not noticed that meanwhile the hail had stopped. I cannot say that everything that crossed my mind while I was falling asleep had disappeared. I did not start having any particular thoughts that were different – some wishes, or plans, or regrets, or anything like that…. But, like any living animal, I was walking… because both my body and my mind knew that walking meant surviving.

It took me another hour and a half to reach the tea house. I could not open the door, but I was able to bang on it with my fist. The hostess who opened took me straight to the fire in the middle of the room. She had me sit on a small stool, not very close to the fire, and wrapped me in some skins. Then she sat next to me and took my hands into hers – to warm them up slowly. After a few minutes I realized that I could not open my mouth. The hostess waited for a long time. Then she told her husband something and he brought a cup of tea. The woman fed me with a teaspoon – slowly, slowly, sip by sip. When I was able to move my lips again, I tried to smile and said thank you – a few times. Sitting at a small table behind my back, there were a few men – my guide and the Sherpa were there too.

"Why didn't you come back with someone to help me?" I asked.

"It was dangerous," he answered. "No one wanted to take the risk. I had to save my own life. I am responsible to show you the way, not to save your life."

"But I won the bet," interrupted another man from the group, someone we had met on the trail the previous day.

"The bet?" I wondered.

"Yeah!" they all agreed in a choir. "He was the only one who said that 'the old woman will make it,' " explained a third man.

I did make it.

Perhaps this was my version of having a second chance. Was I going to change my life, to make up for wasted time, to aim at different goals? To chase after lost dreams? All this never crossed my mind. I was grateful for the life I had, and I was happy to go back to it. And if miraculously I had been rejuvenated or reborn that day and I could have started all over again, I would not have done anything differently.

On the Sandakphu Trek

INDEX

of places and personalities

Judith Wermuth-Atkinson
The Red Jester
Andrei Bely's *Petersburg* As A Novel Of The European Modern
What was Bely's project in his ambiguous novel *Petersburg*? For the first time, this study firmly places Bely's work at the heart of the European Modern (*die Moderne*). It argues that with its concern for the spiritual and its desire to create new aesthetics, the novel helped reshape fundamental views of reality, of the Self, and of consciousness. Theories of Freud and Jung as well as the aesthetics of the Viennese Secession are used to elucidate Bely's approach to the narrative. The author also presents Rudolf Steiner's anthroposophy as the prism through which Bely reflects modernist ideas.
Slavistik, Bd. 1, 2012, 232 S., 29,90 €, br., ISBN-CH 978-3-643-90154-5

Anpassung – Selbstbehauptung – Widerstand

Alice Rühle-Gerstel und Otto Rühle
Tommy's Trip to Mexico – Tommys Reise nach Mexiko
Herausgegeben und mit einem Vorwort versehen von Marta Marková
Otto Rühle, legendärer SPD-Politiker, Marx-Biograph und Mitbegründer des Spartakusbundes, schuf 1941 im mexikanischen Exil gemeinsam mit seiner Ehefrau, der Autorin und Individualpsychologin Alice Rühle-Gerstel, ein Kinderbuch, *Tommys Trip to Mexico*, das Ottos Zeichnungen im Stil des Wiener Kunsthandwerks und Alices Texte vereinen sollte. Der Ausbruch des II. Weltkrieges verhinderte die Herausgabe von *Tommys Trip to Mexico*. Das Buch überlebte nur in Form des Originalmanuskripts und wird nun, gemeinsam mit dem illustrierten Büchlein *Ajijic*, erstmals veröffentlicht.
Bd. 47, 2020, 128 S., 16,80 €, gb., ISBN 978-3-643-50997-0

Willi Feld
Burgsteinfurt während der NS-Zeit
Band 1
Als Ende März 1945 alliierte Truppen die ehemalige Stadt Burgsteinfurt besetzten, war nicht nur ein großer Teil der Innenstadt zerstört. Auch der Ruf der Stadt hatte während der 12 Jahre unter dem NS-Regime stark gelitten. In einem Beitrag der englischen Zeitschrift „The Soldier" wurde sie sogar als „The Village of Hate" tituliert. Die vorliegende, auf insgesamt zwei Bände angelegte, Untersuchung versucht, anhand einer ganzen Reihe paradigmatischer Einzelgeschichten zu zeigen, wie genau sich die nationalsozialistische Herrschaftsform im Mikrokosmos der ehemaligen Stadt Burgsteinfurt realisierte und welche Konsequenzen das für das Leben und Zusammenleben ihrer Einwohner mit sich brachte.
Bd. 46, 2019, 232 S., 24,90 €, br., ISBN 978-3-643-14275-7

Markas Petuchauskas
Der Preis der Eintracht
Memoiren, Künstlerporteräts, kulturelle Interaktionen
„Der Preis der Eintracht" erzählt vom Leben und dem Theater im Wilnaer Getto. Von der Rettung des Autors durch Mitbürger mit Gewissen. Vom Leben als Jude und Intellektueller unter der Sowjetherrschaft und später im wieder freien Litauen. Vom Engagement für das Wiederaufleben der jüdischen Kultur in Vilnius und ganz Litauen sowie dem Einsatz für den Dialog der Kulturen. Der Leser trifft auf weltberühmte und weniger bekannte Litwaken. Und schließlich berichtet Markas Petuchauskas von der exemplarischen Geschichte seiner Familie, deren Mitglieder über die ganze Welt verstreut leben. Ein Buch, das zur Versöhnung und Eintracht aufruft und ihren Preis aufzeigt.
Bd. 45, 2019, 268 S., 44,90 €, br., ISBN 978-3-643-14130-9

Hans-Wilhelm Rahe
Wilhelm Rahe (1896-1976) – westfälischer Pfarrer und Kirchenhistoriker
Ein Leben für Bekenntnis und Menschlichkeit
Im Ersten Weltkrieg Kriegsfreiwilliger, geriet Wilhelm Rahe im Dritten Reich wegen seiner Zugehörigkeit zur Bekennenden Kirche und der Betreuung von Judenchristen in Konflikt mit dem NS-Staat und musste u.a. 20 Vernehmungen und eine Verhaftung durch die Gestapo hinnehmen. Im Zweiten Weltkrieg versorgte er unter Lebensgefahr viele Gemeinden im Kreis Minden. Nach Kriegsende beteiligte er sich maßgeblich am Wiederaufbau der Westfälischen Kirche. Mehr als 30 Jahre war er Vorsitzender des Vereins für Westfälische Kirchengeschichte und Herausgeber der Jahrbücher des Vereins.
Bd. 44, 2019, 96 S., 24,90 €, br., ISBN 978-3-643-14124-8

Roland Girtler; Friederike Okladek-Wilder
Eine Wiener Jüdin im Chor der deutschen Wehrmacht zu Notre-Dame
Dokumentation einer Autobiographie
Bd. 43, 2018, 210 S., 29,80 €, br., ISBN 978-3-643-50853-9

Karl Kohut
Mährische Kindheit, hessische Jugend
Erinnerungen eines Blauäugigen
Bd. 42, 2018, 144 S., 29,90 €, br., ISBN 978-3-643-13912-2

Paula Kienzle
Frauen mit Profil und Tatkraft – in Rottenburg im 20. Jahrhundert
Bd. 41, 2018, 364 S., 19,90 €, br., ISBN 978-3-643-13826-2

Martin Steinacher
Maurice Bavaud – tuer Hitler au nom de la foi catholique ?
Bd. 40, 2017, 136 S., 29,90 €, br., ISBN 978-3-643-13664-0

Bernd Martin; Michael Wernicke (†) (Hg.)
Das Ringen um Religion und Menschlichkeit
Tagebuch des Augustiners Viktor (Erwin) Hümmer –
Wehrmachtssanitäter in Ungarn und während des Warschauer Aufstandes 1944
Bd. 39, 2016, 242 S., 29,90 €, br., ISBN 978-3-643-13354-0

Martin Steinacher
Maurice Bavaud – verhinderter Hitler-Attentäter im Zeichen des katholischen Glaubens?
Bd. 38, 2015, 138 S., 29,90 €, br., ISBN 978-3-643-12932-1

Els Andringa (Hg.)
Avantgarde & Exil – Ludwig Kunz als Kulturvermittler
Autor und Vermittler zwischen den Künsten und Sprachen
Bd. 37, 2017, 326 S., 34,90 €, br., ISBN 978-3-643-90572-7

Ria van den Brandt
Etty Hillesum
An Introduction to Her Thought
Bd. 36, 2014, 152 S., 29,90 €, br., ISBN 978-3-643-90447-8

Leslie Schwartz; Marc David Bonagura
Surviving the Hell of Auschwitz and Dachau
A Teenage Struggle Toward Freedom From Hatred
Bd. 35, 2013, 120 S., 19,90 €, br., ISBN 978-3-643-90368-6

Kurt Mayer; Joe Peterson
Sie nannten mich Israel, aber mein Name ist Kurt
Bd. 34, 2012, 248 S., 39,90 €, gb., ISBN 978-3-643-90269-6

Hans-Karl Seeger; Hermann Hüsken
Dechant Josef Lodde – Coesfelds Fels in der braunen Flut
Christliche Zivilcourage zu Zeit des Nationalsozialismus
Bd. 33, 2011, 176 S., 19,90 €, br., ISBN 978-3-643-11457-0

Ludwig Mehlhorn (Hg.)
Gewissheit im Widerstand
Adam von Trott zum 100. Geburtstag
Bd. 32, 2011, 208 S., 19,90 €, br., ISBN 978-3-643-11422-8